GET YOUR GUIDANCE ON!
A SEL Guidance Curriculum

Stephanie Lerner, MS
Certified School Counselor

Like and follow me on Facebook, Instagram, and the sites below to see my weekly posts on developments in the counseling world and to receive my newest free/low-cost products!

www.schoolcounselorstephanie.com
www.facebook.com/schoolcounselorstephanie
www.instagram.com/schoolcounselorstephanie
www.pinterest.com/schoolcounselorstephanie

For information on this publication or others by this author, visit
www.schoolcounselorstephanie.com
or e-mail the author at
stephanie@schoolcounselorstephanie.com
Special discounts are available on quantity orders.

Table of Contents

Get Your Guidance On:
A Social-Emotional Learning Guidance Curriculum

An Origin Story

After giving students needs assessments over many years, I noticed that they kept requesting guidance on the same topics: they wanted to learn how to improve their grades and how to have overall success in school! So, in the spirit of "giving the people what they want", I began creating lessons for this curriculum. Then, as our students' crisis incidents increased year after year, I wanted to infuse my guidance lessons with mental health support strategies in the hopes of bringing down these crisis numbers and giving students some relief. It worked and the *Get Your Guidance On: A SEL Guidance Curriculum* was born! This book contains lesson plans and activities for August through May of the school year. It also includes a guidance needs assessment and an annual guidance curriculum pre/posttest that can be administered in August and May. The focus of this guidance curriculum is on academic success strategies, mental health support strategies, crisis prevention, and conflict resolution. As a result, you will see activities on these topics in every single lesson in this book. Below is a brief description of each lesson theme with the month it in which it should be taught.

Month, Topics, & Descriptions

August: An Introductory Guidance Lesson- Introduce your role and counseling program to students. In addition to the introductory theme, this lesson comes with a mental health support strategy on handling emergencies, a success in school game, and a guidance curriculum yearly pretest. This lesson also guides students through the Four Steps of Conflict Resolution.

September: Child Abuse Prevention & Awareness- This resource includes an extensive child abuse/neglect prevention and awareness guidance lesson. It gently but powerfully arms students with the info they need to protect themselves and others from harmful situations.

October: Destigmatizing Mental Health Issues- Teach your students that there is nothing unusual or embarrassing about having a mental health issue. This resource teaches students how they can support themselves and others struggling with mental health problems. In addition to the de-stigmatizing theme, it also includes a conflict resolution activity and an academic success strategy with an accompanying weekly grades check sheet.

November: Gratitude- This lesson shows your students how gratitude builds positive feelings. The lesson's themes of appreciation and thankfulness lend it perfectly to the holiday season, as well as any other time that you want students to celebrate gratitude. Using gratitude as a mental health support strategy, it guides students to minimize negative feelings and thoughts. In addition to the gratitude theme, the resource comes with an academic success strategy on backpack organization.

December: Building Hope & Friendship- This lesson explores how building hope and friendship leads to positive mental health. In addition to the hope and friendship themes, the lesson comes with an academic success strategy on notebook organization. Students will also have a chance to role play typical interpersonal conflicts that occur during this busy and exciting time of year.

January: Connecting with Others- This guidance lesson serves as an icebreaker to foster bonding and connection between students. It also explores interpersonal connection as a mental health support strategy. In addition to the icebreaker and connection aspects of this lesson, this resource comes with an academic success strategy of weekly grade check reviews, as well as a conflict resolution activity for typical "winter blues" issues.

February: Are You Life Ready?- Teach your students about college and career readiness (CCR) by exploring the meanings behind being "college ready" and "life ready". The lesson focuses on the financial rewards of post-secondary education as an academic success strategy and on prioritizing tasks as a stress reduction strategy. It includes a conflict resolution role play activity as well.

March: Are You Career Ready?- This guidance lesson teaches students about college and career readiness (CCR) by exploring the meaning of "career ready". It focuses on using technology to find preferred careers and using stress management techniques to help with school/job stressors. The lesson also includes an academic achievement game and a conflict resolution rumor role play.

April: Healthy Eating & Healthy Living for Mental Health- Teach your students that healthy eating is one of the keys to healthy living. It focuses on the dangers of skipping meals as an impediment to good mental health. In addition to the healthy eating piece, it also explores healthy living through academic success and conflict resolution skills. Students will learn how to correctly use a daily planner and how to build up their anti-bullying skills through a bibliocounseling activity.

May: End of Year Guidance Lesson with Needs Assessments & Guidance Posttest - This multi-day guidance lesson uses the book, *I Wish You More,* to guide students in processing their thoughts and feelings about the school year ending. It guides students in exploring their wishes for the future as a mental health support strategy. It also explores academic success and conflict resolution skills: students will learn how to use a college academic tracker and will practice a conflict resolution role play. Finally, use this last guidance lesson to administer the posttest to evaluate student growth and the needs assessment/s to determine areas of focus for the following year. Spend some time this month data mining by comparing your students' results in the pre/posttests.

June/July: NA-SUMMER BREAK

Helpful Tips for Teaching Your Guidance Lessons

This guidance curriculum includes a multi-day guidance lesson for each month of the school year. Each lesson is designed to decrease student problem behaviors (especially crisis incidents) and increase student academic success. In using this guidance curriculum at my own school, we achieved positive gains in both crisis prevention and academic achievement. Following are some helpful tips and resources to assist you on your guidance teaching journey.

Universal Tips

- In each month, a different guidance topic is covered, along with a mental health support strategy, a conflict resolution activity, and an academic success strategy.
- A yearly guidance curriculum pre/posttest is included as well as a needs assessment. Instructions for administering these assessments are included with the assessment resources.
- Guidance lessons are a Tier One support in the Response to Intervention (RTI) and Multi-tiered System of Supports (MTSS) models. This means that every student in the school should receive regularly-occurring guidance lessons (ASCA, 2014). Also, the entire student body needs to see you in guidance lessons, so they know who you are and how to get help from you.
- Each month's lesson can be taught over two 60-minute guidance lesson periods, four 30-minute periods (by dividing each day's activities in half), or even streamlined down to one short lesson. Lessons can be shortened by omitting some of the activities if you have less teaching time or are working with younger group members.
- This curriculum guide is meant to be used in a whole class setting with 15-30 students. However, all of the lessons can be used in the small group setting as well.
- The lessons were developed for students in a school setting, but they can also be modified for use in a clinical setting.
- This is a psychoeducational lessons guide. It should be used to educate students on social-emotional learning skills. It should not be used as a substitute for mental health therapy with a licensed practitioner.
- Collecting guidance lesson data will help you to improve future lessons as well as promote your program with school stakeholders (parents/administrators/staff). Compile, analyze, and present the results of your pre/posttest, needs assessments, and even informal evaluations to your campus administration. More explanation on how to do this is provided with each assessment. In addition, use campus data such as pass/fail grade reports and attendance reports to inform your decisions about the academic or mental health support strategies to focus on. Then, at the end of the year, analyze both your own guidance assessment data as well as the campus data reports in order to determine where your guidance lessons had a positive impact on student success (ASCA, 2016). Finally, present positive student gains to your principal, community, and staff to advocate for future guidance lessons.

Teaching Tips

- Begin every guidance lesson with the following crisis prevention reminders and information (provided in each lesson); these reminders, along with the mental health support strategy that is included with every lesson, will be the key to having a strong crisis prevention program that reduces the number of student crisis incidents.
    - How to see the counselor (utilize request forms for non-emergencies)
    - The "3 hurts emergency" and how to get help
    - All school staff are mandated reporters

- For many years, I worked with a very high crisis school population. To give you an idea, we had 255 student crises (harm to self or another) at my school one year. Unfortunately, counselors across the nation have seen this same unprecedented explosion of student crises over the last ten years (CDC, 2019). If you are interested in the causes behind this tragic trend, I highly recommend the book, *The Coddling of the American Mind*; it really is a must-read for everyone who works with or raises children. If you need more guidance on how to work with high-crisis populations, I have a few different posts/resources on my website that can help- just visit my website at www.schoolcounselorstephanie.com/blog and type the word "crisis" in the search bar there.
- These lessons can be entirely taught by the counselor or co-taught with the counselor beginning the lesson and the teacher following up and finishing the lesson.
- Whether you teach these lessons on your own or with the classroom teacher, it is important to have the teacher in the classroom with you and the students. This is because the teacher's presence is needed to maintain discipline and to make sure that students follow rules- keep in mind that discipline is not your role and is detrimental to the counseling relationship. True confession: When I first started out as a rookie school counselor back in 2008, I thought I'd alleviate some teacher work load, and tell them they didn't need to stick around to discipline during my guidance lessons. Big mistake. I realized pretty quickly that while the kids followed my rules and accepted my consequences for misbehavior, they lost sight of how I could support them. My (inappropriate) role as a disciplinarian, even in a short monthly 30-minute lesson, seriously compromised the way that the students interacted with me as a counselor. In short, they weren't always comfortable coming to me for counseling help because they saw me as their disciplinarian, not as the non-judgmental, always-on-their-side school counselor.
- This resource has various leveled activities, making it appropriate for children in grades three through high school.
- If your students are emerging or struggling readers, consider modifying the activities in these ways: read aloud while students follow along with their finger, shorten or simplify some of the lists/cards, and have students dictate any writing activities or create a template that they can copy rather than writing on their own.
- For teenaged students, remember that the counselor sets the tone for each lesson. Meaning, if you are excited and comfortable with the topic, your teens will come around soon enough and mirror your tone. Likewise, if you feel that certain topics or activities are juvenile and uncomfortable, teens will mirror these feelings too.
- There are a lot of read-aloud opportunities in these sessions- just remind students that they can say "pass" anytime they do not want to read aloud.
- Use the students' responses to the informal evaluations in each class to plan your future lessons. Pay attention to their responses on whether they felt the lesson was enjoyable and clear—if not, consider revising the layout of future lessons or even reteaching that lesson.

Distance Learning

All of the lessons in this book can be modified for the distance learning or virtual classroom by videotaping yourself teaching the lesson and then uploading your video, as well as the needed lesson materials, into your school's FERPA-compliant online platform. Have students watch the video and then do the activities provided for each lesson step. In addition, feel free to skip or modify the interactive parts that do not work for your specific distance learning environment. For example, student pair/group practice activities can be done with a family member instead of a classmate/s; students can then share their home practice experience through a writing summary or video. Similarly, responses to discussion questions can be submitted as written answers or videoclips of their discussions with family members. Alternately, you can use Google Hangouts Meet or another online platform to actually simulate your guidance lesson classroom, where the class meets with you in real time as you teach the lesson. Google has helpful tutorials about this platform and how to set it up. Finally, feel free to remove any activities that don't flow well in the virtual setting. The key in facilitating guidance lessons in the virtual setting is flexibility; with a bit of patience and tweaking, your lessons can run just as effectively in both types of settings.

You can also order other counseling books and resources from my website, www.schoolcounselorstephanie.com.

Get Your Guidance On
A Social-Emotional Learning Guidance Curriculum

August's Theme:
Howdy! An Introductory Guidance Lesson

American School Counselor Association Standards Alignment
Mindsets
M1. Belief in development of whole self, including a healthy balance of mental, social/emotional and physical well-being
Behaviors
B-LS 8. Actively engage in challenging coursework
B-SMS 9. Demonstrate personal safety skills

Objectives
The Student Will:
- Understand the role of the school counselor
- Learn how to how to utilize the school counselor as a mental health support strategy
- Define emergencies and identify how to get help in an emergency situation
- Apply the four steps of peaceful conflict resolution
- Explore various strategies for academic success in school

Materials
School Counselor's Role & Duties info sheet, Student Pre/Postest, pencils, Do You Have an Emergency? posterette, Request to See the Counselor forms/instructions, chart paper, markers, Four Steps of Conflict Resolution posterette, Success in School Bingo, bingo chips, Academic Success Strategies
You'll also need paper plates, tape, and tongue depressors if you are going to play the Never Have I Ever game.

Lesson Steps
DAY ONE

1. Introduction (10 min): Introduce yourself by stating your name, some fun facts about yourself and your role in the school. Ask students what they think your role as school counselor involves.

2. Opening Activity (20 min): Use the attached info sheet School Counselor's Role and Duties to explain the different ways that you support students. Next, read the attached School Counseling Support Statements to the class and have them show thumbs up/down if it is a way that they can enlist school counseling support or not. *Alternately, if you have time, you can turn this into an art activity and game by having students make school counseling support versions of "Never Have I Ever" signs. To do this, give each student a paper plate and tongue depressor. Have students write the phrase "Never will I ever" on one side of their paper plate sign and "I will" on the other side of their sign. Then have them decorate their plates and glue or tape them onto the tongue depressors. Finally read each School Counseling Support Statement and have students show the correct side of their sign to match the statement.*

3. Pretest (5 min): Have the students complete the attached pretest, either electronically (through Google Forms) or in a paper-based form.

4. Mental Health Support Strategy- How to Handle Emergencies (15 min): Ask the class what they think "mental health support strategy" (MHSS) means. Guide them to the idea that it is something they can do or a way to feel better during a rough time; a MHSS promotes positive mental health functioning, which means taking care of our thoughts and feelings so our brain and body work well. Tell students that today's MHSS is about how to get help in an emergency. Have every student tell a partner why it is important to know what to do in an emergency BEFORE the emergency occurs. Next, instruct the class on the following main points related to emergencies:
   - Teach students what defines an emergency by showing the attached Do You Have an Emergency? posterette.
   - Have students brainstorm different situations that could fall into each of the "3 Hurts" emergency categories.
   - Remind students that they should come to your office immediately if they have an emergency and that they don't need to fill out a request form (discussed above in Step 2) for emergencies.
   - Be sure to let students know that all adults in the school building are mandated reporters, which means that they have to enlist the help of another adult (assistant principal, nurse, parent, child protective services, etc.) in an emergency to help keep the student safe.
   - Remind students that they can talk to you about non-emergencies with a counselor request form (attached). Ask students what kinds of non-emergencies they might come to see the counselor about. If time, chart their

responses. Guide them to the idea that they can fill in a request to talk with you about anything they want- friends, school, home, or even just to say "hi!"
- Also, if you will be setting up a weekly Counselor Corner* in the cafeteria, let students know that you are also available to students during lunches on certain days (i.e., Mondays, Wednesdays, and Fridays) so that students can "drop in" and talk to you without a request form.

*Counselor Corner is a set time every week where the counselor sits off to the side in the cafeteria at the counselor corner table during student lunches. At the beginning of every lunch, use the microphone to briefly remind students that you are there to answer any question they have or just to talk; this gives students the opportunity to come up and get to know how you can support them better! It also provides students a chance to get help without filling in a counselor request form.

5. Closure (5 min): Wrap up the lesson by asking students to share their opinions of the following question with a partner: What was the most important thing you learned today?

6. Informal Lesson Evaluation (5 min): End the lesson with a thumbs up-thumbs down evaluation with the class. Have students show a thumbs up or thumbs down as you read them each of the following evaluation statements:
- I understood this lesson.
- I enjoyed this lesson.
- I know how to get immediate help in a "3 Hurts" Emergency.

DAY TWO

1. Introduction (5 min): Introduce or reintroduce yourself by stating your name and your role in the school. Review how students can fill out a Request to See the Counselor form in order to meet with you to talk about any problem they are having. Show the Do You Have an Emergency? posterette to review or explain what defines an emergency. Tell students that they should come to your office immediately if they have an emergency and that they don't need to fill out a request form for emergencies. Remind students that all adults in the building are mandated reporters.

2. Opening Activity (5 min): Ask students why it is important to pass or do well in all their classes and on their tests. Chart their answers and guide them to the idea that passing their classes and state tests helps them to move on to next grade. Explain that school counselors can help with this, especially if students are failing or worried about classes/grades. Remind them to fill out a Request to See the Counselor form if they need academic help or help with a conflict, both of which will be discussed today!

3. Academic Success Strategy- What is Academic Success? (15 min): With the class, briefly summarize the following bulleted ideas:

- A "C" grade or 70% is usually considered a passing grade on a school assignment or test.
- Doing well in school generally means earning grades higher than a "C".
- Students get promoted or advanced to the next grade at the end of the school year when they:
    ✓ Come to school every day and follow the rules.
    ✓ Do their best to pass their classes and turn in all school work.
    ✓ Ask for help every time they need it.

Next, have students use Think-Pair-Share* to brainstorm other strategies to be successful in school. Write their ideas in a list on chart paper and guide the class to the strategies listed in Academic Success Strategies (attached); briefly discuss the meaning of each one as you are listing them on the chart paper. Let the class know that they will be learning more about some of these strategies in future guidance lessons.

Tips for modifying this step: Feel free to skip the first two bullet points and focus on the checkpoints if your students are too young to earn A-F grades. Alternately, if you feel like your students need a more advanced Academic Success Strategy introduction than just Step 3 above, try showing them Harvard consultant Debra Levy's video clip, "Five Strategies for Academic Success" and have students create their own Priority Pie: https://www.extension.harvard.edu/inside-extension/5-strategies-academic-success-using-your-strengths

4. Connection to Day One Activity- Conflict Resolution Introduction (10 min): Ask students, "Did you know that one of the ways to prevent emergencies is to have strong conflict resolution skills?" Ask student to guess why. Show the Conflict Resolution Poster, discuss each step on the poster and how to fill out a counselor or assistant principal request form if a student needs help or if someone is bullying. Ask a few volunteers to try acting out each of the conflict resolution steps while you gently "bother" them (i.e., by tapping a pencil loudly, kicking their chair, cutting in front of them in line, etc.).

5. School Success Bingo (15 min): Play this bingo game with your students for a fun way to wrap up your guidance lesson and apply the academic success strategies. Hand out the attached bingo boards and have students fill in the bolded words from the Academic Success Strategies list (attached) onto their bingo cards. Play the game by following the steps on the attached bingo card.
    If you work with very young students, you might just play a simplified version of the School Success Bingo game. To simplify the game, give students bingo boards that are already filled in with only the first 5-10 strategies from the attached list.

6. Closure (5 min): Wrap up the lesson by asking students to share their opinions of the following question with a partner: What is the academic success strategy that you need to improve on the most?

7. Informal Lesson Evaluation (5 min): End the lesson with a thumbs up-thumbs down evaluation with the class. Have students show a thumbs up or thumbs down as you read them each of the following evaluation statements:
    - I understood this lesson.
    - I enjoyed this lesson.
    - I know some strategies for being successful in school.

Think-Pair-Share strategy: This is a cooperative learning strategy where students work together to answer a question; this strategy requires students to first think silently about the question or topic, second tell a partner their thoughts, and finally share their ideas with the entire class.

School Counselor's Role and Duties

Student Information: Students can talk to their school counselor about feelings, friends, family issues, school, good news, and anything else!! Here is some important information on how school counselors can support students at school...

How to See the Counselor

You can find me at the room number _____, but please submit a "Request to See the Counselor" form before coming to talk to me because I am usually with students. The request forms can be found in the counseling office and you can also get them from your teacher. Turn your completed form in to the counseling office or give it to your teacher. I will talk with you as soon as possible. Only emergencies will be discussed without a request form. An emergency is any of the "3 Hurts":

The 3 Hurts

When you talk to me, I try to keep conversations confidential unless you tell me about the "3 Hurts":

You Hurt Yourself
You Hurt Someone Else
Someone Hurts You (or Another Person)

I also may want to talk to your teacher if you tell me about a school problem, but I will discuss this with you first.

Groups and Individuals

Sometimes I meet with student groups or individuals to discuss/solve problems. Groups run for about 6-8 weeks. Alternately, I only meet with students individually for 2-4 repeating sessions.

Classroom Lessons

Weekly or monthly, I will come to your classroom and spend some class time with you discussing various counseling topics such as personal issues (like stress and anger), college and career information, character education, anti-bullying (including cyberbullying) strategies, good grades tips, and more! During these visits, we will play games, read stories, act out role plays, do creative projects, watch counseling video clips, and more!

School Counseling Support Statements

Counselor Directions: Read each of the following school counseling support statements in a random order to the class. After each statement, the students will show a thumb up/down (or their plate sign) to show their answer regarding if that is a way they can enlist school counseling support or not.
If you are working with elementary students, you may want to remove the last statement from the first list.

I (student) Will:

- Learn about interesting counseling topics in my classroom guidance lesson every week or month.
- Learn about my college and career options.
- Learn ways to stay safe and healthy.
- Explore the world of work.
- Talk to my school counselor if I need their help with a home or school problem.
- Get immediate help from my school counselor if I know of or have an emergency.
- Fill out a request to see the counselor form if I want to talk about a non-emergency issue.
- Be able to talk with my school counselor at the Counselor Corner table during lunch.
- Have the opportunity to participate in a student support group.
- Discuss ways to get good grades.
- Learn about being successful in school.
- Learn some social-emotional learning strategies.
- Check my grades and discuss ways to improve them.
- Get help in selecting my classes.
- Review my credits and graduation options.

Never Will I (student) Ever:

- Have weekly counseling sessions with the school counselor all year.
- Receive therapy from the school counselor.
- Be able to interrupt the school counselor as they work with other students (unless I have an emergency).
- Hang out at the school counselor's house.
- Text the school counselor to their cell phone.
- Learn math from the school counselor.
- Buy lunch from the school counselor.
- Get a discipline referral from the school counselor.
- Get medical care from the school counselor.
- Earn a grade from the school counselor.

Student Yearly Guidance Curriculum Pre/Posttest

Guidance pre/posttests are crucial for providing data on the success of your guidance curriculum; this, in turn, will greatly help you in planning next year's curriculum. Using Google Forms, administer the student pre/posttest at the beginning and end of the school year so it serves as a measure of student knowledge-gained that you can share with your administration and leadership team to advocate for future guidance curriculum opportunities. You can also administer the pretest below in the form of a paper-based survey which works well too, though it is much more time-consuming to analyze and compile paper-based data. The questions on the pre/posttest reflect the main points to teach students during guidance lessons throughout the year.

Counselor Directions:
Administer the pretest in your first guidance lesson of the school year by reading each question aloud to the class as students independently mark their response to the question. Next, analyze the pretest data. The posttest can be administered during the last guidance lesson of the year, or sometime later in May/June right before the students leave for summer break. At that point, you will be able to compile the posttest data; then compare the data from both the pretest and posttest to share those findings with your admin team in order to advocate and plan for your counseling program.
**If you are using these resources with younger students, consider trimming them down by half and removing the statements that may not apply to your age group.*
On the next page is the pretest to use; feel free to print it out and use as is or turn it into a Google Form, Survey Monkey, or any other medium of your choice. Happy Data Collecting!

Student Pre/Posttest

<u>Student Directions</u>: Here are some questions for you to answer about our counseling program. Your counselors want to help you as much as possible, so please answer each question honestly by circling or marking your response.
Thank you!

	PRETEST			QUESTIONS	POSTTEST		
1.	YES	NO	NOT SURE	Do you know what your counselor's name is?	YES	NO	NOT SURE
2.	YES	NO	NOT SURE	Do you know what jobs your counselor does at school?	YES	NO	NOT SURE
3.	YES	NO	NOT SURE	Do you know where the counseling office is?	YES	NO	NOT SURE
4.	YES	NO	NOT SURE	If you have an emergency, do you know how get to your counselor right away?	YES	NO	NOT SURE
5.	YES	NO	NOT SURE	Do you know how to fill out a *Request to See the Counselor* form?	YES	NO	NOT SURE
6.	YES	NO	NOT SURE	Do you think most people have mental health problems sometime in their life?	YES	NO	NOT SURE
7.	YES	NO	NOT SURE	Do you know how to get help if you are bullied?	YES	NO	NOT SURE
8.	YES	NO	NOT SURE	Has the counselor talked to you/your class about how to be successful in school?	YES	NO	NOT SURE
9.	YES	NO	NOT SURE	Can you state at least three strategies for improving your grades in school?	YES	NO	NOT SURE
10.	YES	NO	NOT SURE	Has the counselor talked to you/your class about college and careers?	YES	NO	NOT SURE

Request to See the Counselor

Virtual Requests to See the Counselor

It is crucial to tell students the protocol for how they can access you and request an appointment with you. I start off all guidance lessons with a reminder to students of how I can support them. During this reminder, I make sure they understand that they must request an appointment with me through request forms (for non-emergencies).

Now, for students that need to talk in a virtual school counseling setting, I think it is best to have them email or (even better) have them fill out a Google form- it's easy to set up; Google has helpful steps and a tutorial on how to do this. Here are some tips:

- Provide an intro and instructions with your google form, something like this:

  Students should email their counselor if they need help with a counseling issue. You can also "meet" with me by signing up for a time below. I'll send you an invite with the time that we will meet in Google hangouts. You'll need to have your Google Hangout app downloaded to your phone/device to be able to use it so we can "meet." Remember the "3 Hurts"! If there is a concern that you may harm yourself or others, or that someone is causing you harm, I will notify the appropriate persons. Also, confidentiality cannot be guaranteed in virtual meetings due to the nature of the "cloud".

- You can also videotape yourself telling students this italicized info above as well as posting it on your website and the homepage of your online platform.
- I've attached my paper request form below in case you need a template for what to include in your Google Form.
- Google Hangouts is a great platform so that you can meet with the student. Take some time to set it up and then practice using it with a family member or a colleague first, just so you have it down.

Paper Requests to See the Counselor

Request to See the Counselor Form
Name _____ Grade _____ Date _____
Optional Comments:
*Please be careful about what information you include below because this form may not be confidential.
_____
_____

Do You Have an Emergency?

An emergency usually involves one or more of the following "3 Hurts" situations:

❖ You want to physically hurt yourself.

❖ You want to physically hurt someone else.

❖ Someone threatens to physically hurt you (or someone else).

If you have one of these "3 Hurts", tell your counselor or another trusted adult right away!!!

The 4 Steps of Conflict Resolution

1.   **Ignore**

2.   **Walk Away**

3.   **Use an "I" message**
     Examples:
     ✓ **I wish you wouldn't you kick my chair.**
     ✓ **I don't like it when write about me on Instagram.**

4.   **Tell an Adult**

Academic Success Strategies

- Set **goals** for yourself!
- Follow school **rules**.
- Do your **homework**.
- Do your **classwork.**
- **Ask** for help.
- Ask **questions** if you don't understand.
- Organize your **backpack** every week.
- **Attend** school daily.
- Have a good **study place** at home.
- Be **on-time** to school.
- Have all your **materials** for class.
- Show good **body language** in class.
- **Participate** in class.
- Use a student **planner**.
- Keep your schoolwork in a **binder**.

School Success Bingo

Student Instructions:

- Your counselor will call out a bingo letter and success strategy.
- If you have that combination of bingo letter and strategy, put a bingo chip in the correct spot on your bingo card.
- If you get five bingo chips placed in a row or column, call out "BINGO", so you can win a prize.
- To play a second game, your counselor may have you clear your card of game pieces and start again.
- After the game, the counselor will collect the bingo cards to be used again for a future game.

B	I	N	G	O
		FREE SPACE		

September's Theme:
Child Abuse Prevention & Awareness

American School Counselor Association Standards Alignment
Mindsets
M1. Belief in development of whole self, including a healthy balance of mental, social/emotional and physical well-being
Behaviors
B-SMS 9. Demonstrate personal safety skills
B-SS 3. Create relationships with adults that support success

Objectives
The Student Will:
- Define child abuse and identify its various types
- Explore ways to get help for child abuse as a mental health support strategy
- Review emergency criteria and identify how to get help in an emergency situation
- Apply the four steps of peaceful conflict resolution
- Play Success in School bingo in order to review strategies for academic success in school

Child Abuse Prevention & Awareness- The Law
Child abuse awareness and prevention is often a tough topic to broach with children. However, our number one priority is to keep them safe. As a result, most states have laws mandating that this kind of information is shared with school-aged children. Here is an example- below are the laws in Texas mandating that students must be taught abuse prevention and awareness.
Sec. 38.004. CHILD ABUSE REPORTING AND PROGRAMS.
(b) Each school district shall provide child abuse anti-victimization programs in elementary and secondary schools.
Sec. 38.0041. POLICIES ADDRESSING SEXUAL ABUSE AND OTHER MALTREATMENT OF CHILDREN.
(b) A policy required by this section must address:
(1) methods for increasing staff, student, and parent awareness of issues regarding sexual abuse, sex trafficking, and other maltreatment of children, including prevention

techniques and knowledge of likely warning signs indicating that a child may be a victim of sexual abuse, sex trafficking, or other maltreatment, using resources developed by the agency under Section 38.004 or by the commissioner under Section 28.017;
(2) actions that a child who is a victim of sexual abuse, sex trafficking, or other maltreatment should take to obtain assistance and intervention; and
(3) available counseling options for students affected by sexual abuse, sex trafficking, or other maltreatment.

Note to Counselor

Child abuse/neglect may be a difficult topic for some of your students, especially those that are experiencing family problems or changes. Consult with your co-counselor and/or administrator about how best to prepare students for this lesson or to address any students that get upset during the lesson. Always inform your admin before teaching this lesson. It is important to teach this lesson despite its sensitive (and possibly upsetting) nature-- child abuse education breaks the cycle of abuse.

Materials
- Get Help strategies list, Child Abuse Vocabulary, Child Abuse Statistic Cards, chart paper, markers, crayons, blank white paper, pencils, bingo chips
- Printables from the August Lesson: Do You Have an Emergency? posterette, Request to See the Counselor forms/instructions, 4 Steps of Conflict Resolution posterette, Academic Success Strategies, School Success Bingo

Lesson Steps
DAY ONE

*This is a 90 minute lesson in order to gently ease students into this disturbing topic. Feel free to remove the statistics and conflict resolution steps if you are short on time.

1. Introduction (5 min): Introduce or re-introduce yourself by stating your name and your role in the school. Discuss how students can fill out a Request to See the Counselor form in order to meet with you to talk about any problem they are having, use the attached request forms/instructions if necessary. Show the Do You Have an Emergency? poster to review or explain what defines an emergency. Tell students that they should tell you or another adult immediately if they have an emergency and that they don't need to fill out a request form for emergencies. Remind students that all school staff must report "3 hurts" emergencies to another adult (parent, counselor, assistant principal, etc.) in order to keep students safe.

2. Opening Activity (10 min): Tell students that one of the types of emergencies that children might have to deal with is child abuse. Ask the class if anyone can give a definition of child abuse. Guide students to the idea that child abuse occurs when an adult causes physical injury, death, emotional harm or threat of serious injury to a

child. Tell students that today they will be learning about the kinds of child abuse that exist and how to get help if they or someone they know is experiencing abuse.

3. Instruction (30 min): Hand out the child abuse statistics cards to various students. Have each student read their card while the rest of the class shows if they think the stat is true (thumb up) or false (thumb down). After, tell the class that all the stats are true!! Ask the class why it is important that they learn about this upsetting topic (*answer: so they know what kind of behavior is considered abuse and how to get help for it*). Next, show the class the child abuse vocabulary and organize the students into small groups. Assign each group a vocabulary word/phrase and have them work together to define it. Have each group share their definition and then discuss if that definition is accurate based on the attached definitions.

4. Mental Health Support Strategy- How to Get Help (15 min): Give the class think time to come up with ways to get help if they or someone they know is being abused or neglected. Write their answers on chart paper. Add any of the attached Get Help ideas that are not already on the chart paper from the students.

5. Conflict Resolution Practice (10 min): Wind down this heavy lesson in a lighthearted way with a conflict resolution role play. Teach or review the 4 Steps of Conflict Resolution posterette with the class. Then, choose one student volunteer to act out the 4 Steps of Conflict Resolution while you gently "bother" them (i.e., kick their chair or tap your pencil annoyingly).

6. Closure (5 min): Have students share the most important fact they learned in today's lesson.

7. Informal Lesson Evaluation (5 min): End the lesson with a quick class evaluation. Have students do a thumbs up-thumbs down lesson evaluation with you while you read them each of the following statements:
   - I understood today's lesson.
   - I know what child abuse is.
   - I know what neglect is.
   - I can identify the four types of child abuse.

DAY TWO

1. Introduction (5 min): Re-introduce yourself by stating your name and your role in the school. Review how students can fill out a Request to See the Counselor form in order to meet with you to talk about any problem they are having, use the attached request forms/instructions if necessary. Show the Do You Have an Emergency? poster to review what defines an emergency. Tell students that they should tell you or another adult immediately if they have an emergency and that they don't need to fill out a request form for emergencies. Remind students that all school staff must report "3 hurts" emergencies to another adult (parent, counselor, assistant principal, etc.) in order to keep students safe.

2. Opening Activity (5 min): Briefly review the definition of child abuse with the class (child abuse occurs when a parent or caregiver causes physical injury, death, emotional harm or threat of serious injury to a child). Tell students that today they will do an art project about how to get help if they or someone they know is experiencing abuse.

3. Connection to Day One Activity- Get Help Art Activity (30 min): Briefly review the Get Help strategies that students generated in the last lesson and have students pick the one they think would be most effective. Next, hand out blank paper, pencils, crayons, and markers to students. Tell the students they will be doing an art activity related to getting help and then model each of the steps of the art activity:
   ✓ Write the Get Help strategy name as a title at the top of the paper.
   ✓ Illustrate the strategy in the middle of the paper.
   ✓ Write a sentence explaining the strategy at the bottom of the paper.
   Once you are done modeling, have each student do their own Get Help art project. When everyone is done, lead the class on a walk around the classroom so that they can see all the illustrated ways to get help for child abuse/neglect.

4. Academic Success Strategy- School Success Bingo (15 min): Use a School Success Bingo game to end this lesson on a fun and lighthearted note. Make bingo cards (see attached directions) or hand out the bingo cards that students made in the last guidance lesson; follow the steps on the attached bingo card to play. *If you work with very young children, you might just play a simplified version of the School Success Bingo game. To simplify the game, give students bingo boards that are already filled in with only the first 5-10 strategies from the attached list. Go over the strategies with them before the game to briefly explain each one.*

5. Closure (5 min): Wrap up the lesson by fostering a brief discussion on how they felt during these lessons on child abuse and prevention. Use the questions below to guide the discussion:
   • How did you feel while learning about this topic?
   • Explain why you liked or disliked this lesson.
   • What would you do if you saw or heard about a student being abused?

6. Informal Lesson Evaluation (5 min): End the lesson with a thumbs up-thumbs down evaluation with the class. Have students show a thumbs up or thumbs as you read them each of the following evaluation statements:
   • I understood this lesson.
   • I know what child abuse is.
   • I know how to get help if I or someone I know experiences abuse.

Child Abuse Statistics Cards

Child abuse affects 700,000 children in the US each year.	Children from all religions, ethnic groups, and cultures are affected by child abuse.
Most child abuse victims suffer from neglect, rather than abuse.	More than 90% of child sexual abuse victims know their abuser.
Child Protective Services helps more than 3 million children each year.	More than half of child abusers are women.
On average, four out of five times, abusers are the victim's parents.	Boys are more often the victim of child abuse than girls.

(AmericanSPCC.org, 2019)

Child Abuse Vocabulary

Physical Abuse

A physical injury or threat of a physical injury that causes serious harm to the child (such as punching, beating, shaking, kicking, hitting, burning, etc.)

Neglect

When a parent or caregiver does not take care of their child's basic needs, such as medical, food, shelter, and clothing (this excludes failure caused by financial inability unless services have been offered and refused by parent/caregiver).

Sexual Abuse

Harming a child by: touching any of the areas a bathing suit covers, involving them in indecent exposure, or exposing them to pornographic materials.

Emotional Abuse

Causing mental or emotional injury that impairs the child's growth, development, or psychological functioning.

Get Help Strategies

❖ Tell yourself and your friends that no one has the right to abuse anyone, no one deserves to be abused, and it is never the victim's fault.

❖ Know that victims are not alone- many children experience and find help for child abuse/neglect.

❖ Tell a trusted adult- teacher, coach, parent, counselor, school nurse, etc.

❖ If necessary, keep telling adults until someone believes and helps you!

❖ Call 911 and tell about the abuse/neglect.

❖ Talk to a ChildHelp hotline counselor: it is free to call **1-800-4-A-CHILD (1-800-422-4453).**

❖ Do not be alone with anyone who hurts you.

❖ Listen to your inner voice if it tells you something that is happening to you isn't right.

October's Theme:
Destigmatizing Mental Health Issues

American School Counselor Association Standards Alignment
Mindsets
M1. Belief in development of whole self, including a healthy balance of mental, social/emotional and physical well-being
Behaviors
B-LS 4. Apply self-motivation and self-direction to learning
B-SMS 9. Demonstrate personal safety skills
B-SS 4. Demonstrate empathy

Objectives
The student will:
- Identify ways to support others with mental health issues
- Explore academic success as a mental health support strategy
- Develop strategies to check and improve their grades each week
- Define emergencies and identify how to get help in an emergency situation
- Apply the four steps of peaceful conflict resolution

Materials
- Destigmatizing Mental Health Issues, chart paper, markers, internet with projector to show class some Google images, Warning Signs of Mental Health Problems, scrap paper, pencils, computer with grade software loaded or Weekly Grade Sheet
- Printables from the August's Lesson: Do You Have an Emergency? posterette, Request to See the Counselor forms/instructions, 4 Steps of Conflict Resolution posterette

Lesson Steps:
DAY ONE

1. Introduction (5 min): Re-introduce yourself by stating your name and your role in the school. Review how students can fill out a Request to See the Counselor form in order to meet with you to talk about any problem they are having, use the attached request forms/instructions if necessary. Show the Do You Have an Emergency?

poster to review what defines an emergency. Tell students that they should tell you or another adult immediately if they have an emergency and that they don't need to fill out a request form for emergencies. Remind students that all school staff must report "3 hurts" emergencies to another adult (parent, counselor, assistant principal, etc.) in order to keep students safe.

2. Opening Activity (10 min): Ask students to stand up if they got sick with a cold or a cough in the last year. Now ask them to sit down if they felt embarrassed about having a cold or a cough. Point out that few or no students sat down because everyone understands that having a physical illness like a cold or cough is a normal of being human- it happens to everyone! Chart students' ideas on the following question: When you think of mental illness, what words come to mind? After charting their responses, tell them that mental health problems affect a physical part of the body (YOUR BRAIN) just like any other medical problem! Explain that this means that there is no more reason to be embarrassed about having a mental health problem than by having a cold or cough!

3. Mental Health Support Strategy- Destigmatizing Mental Health Issues (30 min): Use the attached Destigmatizing Mental Health Issues sheet for the following activities:
   - Show or read the following statistics from the attached Destigmatizing Mental Health Issues sheet one at a time. After reading each stat, have the class show a thumb up if they think the statement is true or a thumb down if they think the statement is false. After sharing all statements, tell class all are true!!
   - Ask students what "destigmatize" means and guide them to the idea that to destigmatize something is to remove any shame associated with it. Ask them why it might be important to destigmatize mental health issues. Explain that when people are not embarrassed about their mental health, they will seek help if they need it! Motivate students to action with the following statement: "Let's de-stigmatize mental health problems together by supporting each other and asking for help! Asking for help early on prevents '3 Hurts' Emergencies!"
   - Using Google images, find and show online photos of the attached list of famous musicians, athletes, and actors. Ask students to stand if they think the person has a mental health illness. After showing all pictures, tell the class that every person shown has/had a mental health issue! Ask students, "So what can we do to support ourselves or others who are struggling with mental health issues?"
   - Show the attached info sheet called Warning Signs of Mental Health Problems and briefly discuss each one. Tell students that if they see any of these signs in themselves/others and are worried, they should talk to their counselor right away. Let students know that catching mental health issues early is how we prevent "3 hurts" emergencies!
   - Let students know that they will do a followup application activity on this topic in the next guidance lesson.

4. Closure (5 min): Wrap up the lesson by asking students to share their opinions of the following question with a partner: Why is it important that we work together to support people struggling with mental health issues?

5. Informal Lesson Evaluation (5 min): End the lesson with a thumbs up-thumbs down evaluation with the class. Have students show a thumb up/down as you read them each of the following evaluation statements:
   - I understood this lesson.
   - I enjoyed this lesson.
   - I know that having a mental health issue is a normal part of being a human.

DAY TWO

1. Introduction (5 min): I Re-introduce yourself by stating your name and your role in the school. Review how students can fill out a Request to See the Counselor form in order to meet with you to talk about any problem they are having, use the attached request forms/instructions if necessary. Show the Do You Have an Emergency? poster to review what defines an emergency. Tell students that they should tell you or another adult immediately if they have an emergency and that they don't need to fill out a request form for emergencies. Remind students that all school staff must report "3 hurts" emergencies to another adult (parent, counselor, assistant principal, etc.) in order to keep students safe.

2. Opening Activity (5 min): Ask all students to stand. Tell them to stay standing if they know one way to help someone struggling with a mental health issue/sit down if they don't. Second, tell them to stay standing if they think getting good grades helps their mental health/sit down if grades have nothing to do with mental health. Finally, tell them to stay standing if they think conflict resolution can help their mental health/sit down if conflict resolution doesn't help mental health. Tell the class that today we will learn about mental health supports in the form of academic success and conflict resolution.

3. Connection to Day One Activity- Snowball (10 min): Hand out scrap paper and ask students to write down the most important thing they learned in the last lesson about destigmatizing mental health issues (if a lot of time has gone by between Day One and Day Two of this guidance lesson, then you may need to review the main points that you covered in Day One). Have everyone crumple up their paper and throw it into the center of the room. Then each student should pick up one of the "snowballs" that isn't theirs and read it aloud to the group. This will serve as a fun and motivating whole class review of the Day One topics.

4. Academic Success Strategy- Weekly Grade Checks (20 min): Briefly discuss with students that doing well in school academically helps them to feel good about themselves, which, in turn, boosts their mental health. Remind the class that school counselors can help if students are failing or worried about classes/grades. Tell

students that today you will teach them an academic success strategy that will help them to boost their grades! If your students have access to a software or online program that tracks their grades, show them how to use this. For example, my school uses the computer system, Skyward, so I just demonstrate the software tutorial to show students how to access and review their grades and assignments. I show them how to interpret their weekly grade averages with all the assignments listed that contribute to that average. Alternately, if your school doesn't have a computerized grade system, you can pass out and show students how to use the attached Weekly Grade Sheet to review their grades each week.
If you work with young students who are not yet earning grades, you might skip #3 or do the alternate attached activity, Do You Have a Study Spot?

5. Conflict Resolution Practice (15 min). Ask students, "How might having strong conflict resolution skills help you support someone with a mental health issue? What if the person with the mental health issue is you- how will having conflict resolution skills allow you to help yourself out?" Show the Conflict Resolution Poster, review the poster steps and how to fill out a counselor request form if adult help is needed. Ask a few volunteers to try acting out each of the conflict resolution steps while you "bother" them by acting in an irrational manner (i.e., becoming enraged over a small misunderstanding). After the role play, process the activity with a few guiding questions such as:
   - What went well in this role play?
   - What would be hard for you if you encountered this type of student conflict?
   - What are some other ways you might resolve this type of conflict?

6. Closure (10 min): Wrap up the lesson by asking students to tell their neighbor one thing they can do to help if they suspect that a friend or family member is having a mental health issue. Discuss responses with the class, leading them to ideas such as, tell them you care, offer to accompany them to the school counselor, get help from a trusted adult, listen non-judgmentally, offer to spend time with them, etc.

7. Lesson Evaluation (5 min): End the lesson with a thumbs up-thumbs down evaluation with the class. Have students show a thumbs up or thumbs as you read them each of the following evaluation statements:
   - I understood this lesson.
   - I enjoyed this lesson.
   - I know how to check on my grades once a week and to get help do if they are low.

Destigmatizing Mental Health Issues

Counselor Info to Share with Students

The Stats!

 ➢ 1 in 5 children, aged 13-18, have or will have a mental health problem.
 ➢ 50% of all lifetime cases of mental illness begin by age 14 and 75% by age 24.
 ➢ Approximately 50% of students age 14 and older with a mental illness drop out of high school.
 ➢ 70% of youth in state and local juvenile justice systems have a mental illness (NAMI.org, 2019).

Did You Know?

Each of the following famous people has battled mental health issue and with treatment, they live happy, healthy, successful lives!

Feel free to show as many or as few images of these people to your students, based on student age, understanding, and interests.

 ➢ Serena Williams, tennis player, depression
 ➢ Hope Solo, soccer player, depression
 ➢ Kendall Jenner, model ,anxiety
 ➢ Christy Teigen, model, post-partum depression
 ➢ Andrew Johns, Australian soccer player, Bi polar disorder (BPD)
 ➢ Charles Haley, Dallas Cowboy, BPD
 ➢ Ryan Tedder, One Republic singer, anxiety
 ➢ Delonte West, basketball player, BPD
 ➢ Pete Wentz, Fall Out Boy singer, BPD
 ➢ Lady Gaga, singer, PTSD
 ➢ J.K. Rowling, Harry Potter series author, depression
 ➢ Janet Jackson, singer, depression
 ➢ Demi Lovato, singer, bulimia and BPD
 ➢ Ricky Williams, singer, social anxiety disorder
 ➢ Catherine Zeta-Jones, actress, BPD
 ➢ Jim Carrey, actor, depression (Prevention.com, 2019)

Warning Signs of Mental Health Problems

<u>Counselor Directions:</u> Tell students that if they see any of these signs in themselves/others and are worried, they should talk to their counselor right away. Let students know that catching mental health issues early is how we prevent "3 hurts" emergencies.

- **Extreme mood swings**

- **Verbal or physical aggression**

- **Self-harm**

- **Extreme interest in death or violence**

- **Sudden worsening in school, grades**

- **Withdrawal from friends and extracurricular activities**

- **Repeated expressions of sadness, hopelessness, anger**

- **Lots of Indecision, lack of concentration, and forgetfulness**

- **Talking or writing about suicide or death**

- **Dropping out of social, athletic, and/or community activities (Mayo Clinic, 2018)**

Weekly Grade Sheet

<u>Counselor Directions</u>: If your school doesn't have a computerized grade system, you can use the Weekly Grade Sheet. It is a more time-consuming option with less comprehensive data, but at least your students will have weekly access to their grade averages. During the guidance lesson, hand out a Weekly Grade Sheet to each student and model how to complete it with their teacher; it is best to have a student volunteer act as the teacher/s while you talk to the student-volunteer-acting-as-teacher to show the class how to have a brief conversation with their teacher/s, fill it the sheet themselves, and then ask the teacher to initial their entry.

Weekly Grade Sheet for _____ **Date:** _____

1st Period and/or Subject:	Grade Average:	Comments (Reasons for Failing Average, if Applicable):	Teacher Signature:
2nd Period and/or Subject:	Grade Average:	Comments (Reasons for Failing Average, if Applicable):	Teacher Signature:
3rd Period and/or Subject:	Grade Average:	Comments (Reasons for Failing Average, if Applicable):	Teacher Signature:
4th Period and/or Subject:	Grade Average:	Comments (Reasons for Failing Average, if Applicable):	Teacher Signature:
5th Period and/or Subject:	Grade Average:	Comments (Reasons for Failing Average, if Applicable):	Teacher Signature:
6th Period and/or Subject:	Grade Average:	Comments (Reasons for Failing Average, if Applicable):	Teacher Signature:

Do You Have a Study Spot?

<u>Counselor Directions:</u> Ask students why it is important to have a study or homework spot at home. Next ask them what they should do in their study spot. Lead them to the ideas in the passage below.

It's important to have a good place to study at home where you can do your homework, read a book, study, or do any other task that the teacher tells you to do or that you think will help you learn. A "good place" means somewhere that is quiet, orderly, well-lit, full of the supplies you need, and free of distractions. Politely explain to your family that when you're sitting at your study spot, they should help you get your work done by not distracting you.

Now have students sit in a circle and show the following questions on chart paper or on the board. Go around the circle, giving each student a chance to answer the question or say pass. Once a student answers the question, the student on their left will state if they agree/disagree with the answer and then add their own ideas to the answer. Everyone who contributes an answer (right or wrong) gets a bean or chip. Everyone with a bean or chip at the end of the activity, gets to trade that bean/chip into you for a decoration or supply to add to their home study spot (i.e., sticker, bookmark, pencil, etc.)

- ✓ *How do you ignore and handle distractions at school?*
- ✓ *How could you use the above school anti-distraction strategies at home?*
- ✓ *What are some ways family members (including pets!) can distract someone in their study spot.*
- ✓ *If you have a study spot, describe it. If you don't have a study spot, what would you like yours to have?*
- ✓ *What could be hard about having a home study spot? Why?*
- ✓ *What could be fun about having a home study spot? Why?*
- ✓ *If you have one, rate your study place at home on a scale of 1-10, with 10 being the best. Why did you give it that number?*
- ✓ *If you don't have a study spot, what do you think a "10" study spot has?*
- ✓ *Do you have a family member or friend who has a study spot? Describe it.*

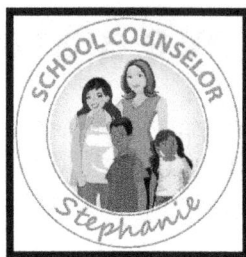

November's Theme:
Having an Attitude of Gratitude

American School Counselor Association Standards Alignment
Mindsets
M 6. Positive attitude toward work and learning
Behaviors
B-SMS 9. Demonstrate personal safety skills
B-LS 3. Use time-management, organizational and study skills

Objectives
The student will:
- Identify gratitude as a way to minimize negative feelings and increase positive feelings.
- Explore gratitude as a mental health support strategy.
- Practice strategies to keep their backpack neat and organized each week.
- Define emergencies and identify how to get help in an emergency situation.
- Apply the four steps of peaceful conflict resolution to a minor family holiday conflict.

Materials
- An Attitude of Gratitude Handout with "Thankful" poem, sticky notes or notecards, clipboards, beans or chips for playing The Gratitude Game, chart paper, markers, pencils, paper, Backpack Organizational Checklists, sample disorganized backpack to organize in demo
- Printables from the August's Lesson: Do You Have an Emergency? posterette, Request to See the Counselor forms/instructions, 4 Steps of Conflict Resolution posterette

Lesson Steps
DAY ONE

1. Introduction (5 min): Re-introduce yourself by stating your name and your role in the school. Review how students can fill out a Request to See the Counselor form in order to meet with you to talk about any problem they are having, use the attached request forms/instructions if necessary. Show the Do You Have an Emergency?

poster to review what defines an emergency. Tell students that they should tell you or another adult immediately if they have an emergency and that they don't need to fill out a request form for emergencies. Remind students that all school staff must report "3 hurts" emergencies to another adult (parent, counselor, assistant principal, etc.) in order to keep students safe.

2. Opening Activity (10 min): Read students the attached Thankful poem and ask them why Americans celebrate the Thanksgiving holiday. Guide them to the idea that it is an opportunity to spend time with loved ones and reflect on what we are grateful, or thankful, for in our lives.

3. Mental Health Support Strategy- An Attitude of Gratitude (30 min): With this strategy, you will show the class that feeling gratitude each day can minimize the amount of negative feelings people have like sadness, anger, etc. Explanations, resources, and steps for this mental health support strategy are attached after this lesson.

4. Closure (5 min): Wrap up the lesson by asking students to share their opinions of the following question with a partner: Why is it important that we develop a habit of noticing things that we are grateful for each day? Have the class discuss their ideas on this question briefly.

5. Informal Lesson Evaluation (5 min): Have students show a thumbs up or thumbs down as you read them each of the following evaluation statements:
   - I understood this lesson.
   - I enjoyed this lesson.
   - I know some ways to use gratitude to decrease my negative feelings.

DAY TWO

1. Introduction (5 min): Re-introduce yourself by stating your name and your role in the school. Review how students can fill out a Request to See the Counselor form in order to meet with you to talk about any problem they are having, use the attached request forms/instructions if necessary. Show the Do You Have an Emergency? poster to review what defines an emergency. Tell students that they should tell you or another adult immediately if they have an emergency and that they don't need to fill out a request form for emergencies. Remind students that all school staff must report "3 hurts" emergencies to another adult (parent, counselor, assistant principal, etc.) in order to keep students safe.

2. Opening Activity (5 min): Have students brainstorm a list of the most common items they use in their everyday lives and why they appreciate having these items. Write a list of the common items they generate on chart paper.

3. Connection to Day One Activity- The Gratitude Game (15 min): Begin The Gratitude Game by having the students sit in a circle. Put the chart paper list of common items

in the middle of the circle. Give each student a bean or chip and, moving in a clockwise position starting with the youngest person in the room, have each student take a turn to toss their chip onto the chart paper- the student must then tell how they would feel or function without that object (that the bean/chip landed on) in their life. After the game, foster a brief discussion on how different life might be without these common items, how other people in the world live without some of these items, and how grateful we are to have them.

4. Academic Success Strategy- Organizing Your Backpack (20 min): Briefly discuss with students that a well-organized backpack is their main tool for doing well in school since it is the place to keep everything needed to complete and submit school assignments. Tell them that their academic strategy today is to clean out their backpack regularly and you will show them an efficient and easy way to do it! Follow the instructions in the attached Academic Success Strategy pages.

5. Conflict Resolution Practice (10 min): Explain that during this time of year, it is natural for family conflicts to occur. Ask students to share some ideas over how they can be resolved. Follow the steps on the attached Conflict Resolution at Family Events page to give students more tools and tips on this topic.

6. Closure (5 min): Wrap up the lesson by asking students what they are going to be most grateful for during the upcoming Thanksgiving holiday. Allow them to share their answers with the class.

7. Lesson Evaluation (5 min): End the lesson with a thumbs up-thumbs down evaluation with the class. Have students show a thumbs up or thumbs down as you read them each of the following evaluation statements:
   - I understood this lesson.
   - I enjoyed this lesson.
   - I know the steps to keeping my backpack well-organized.

Having an Attitude of Gratitude

Counselor Info to Share with Students

Thankful Poem by Mandy Cidlik
No ghosts or goblins and trick-or-treats,
No candy or flowers for your sweets.
No gifts to buy or presents to give,
Just be THANKFUL for the life that you live.

Gratitude Definition
What is gratitude? It is the quality of feeling appreciative and thankful, which leads to personal contentment and goodwill towards others.

Gratitude: The Research
"Gratitude improves psychological health. Gratitude reduces a multitude of toxic emotions, from envy and resentment to frustration and regret. Robert Emmons, a leading gratitude researcher, has conducted multiple studies on the link between gratitude and well-being. His research confirms that gratitude effectively increases happiness and reduces depression" (Morin, 2015, para. 4).

An Attitude of Gratitude

<u>Counselor Directions</u>: Practicing daily gratitude is a mental health support strategy that all students can benefit from learning. Introduce this strategy by telling the class that mental health researchers believe feeling gratitude each day can minimize the amount of negative feelings people have like sadness, anger, etc. If you work with older students, you can even share the attached research. Discuss with students that when we use gratitude to minimize negative feelings, it is a form of crisis prevention.

Lead students through one of the following gratitude-strengthening activities by following the steps below.

Steps
1. Begin by showing the class this quote: "Have an attitude of gratitude."
2. Next, define gratitude with the class (use previous definition, if needed).
3. Once students understand the meaning of the word gratitude, ask them to discuss the possible meaning of the quote with a partner. Have partners share out their quote meanings.
4. Have the class complete one of the following gratitude activities (or all three if you want to extend this lesson into a unit). For best results, follow these tasks in order:
   - Review the activity instructions first with the class.
   - Model the instructions, showing students how to do each of the activity steps.
   - Lead students through the activity, having them complete it as you guide them.
   - Finally process the activity with a few guiding questions, such as:
     - ✓ What did you like best about this activity?
     - ✓ What did you like least about this activity?
     - ✓ How did the activity make you feel?
     - ✓ How could this activity help someone minimize negativity?

Gratitude Activity Options

Option 1: A Sense of Gratitude

This soothing activity combines the mindfulness practice of grounding with gratitude. Here are the activity instructions:

- ➢ Ask students to relax in a seated position and take a few deep breaths.
- ➢ Then, ask them to think about or say out loud:
  - o 3 things they are grateful to see,
  - o 2 things they are grateful to hear,
  - o 1 thing they are grateful to smell.

  *They can use their senses in the moment or use a past sense they have been grateful to experience.

Option 2: It's Better in a Letter

Have students think of someone they are grateful to have in their lives. Ask a few students to share who their person is with the class. Next, have each student write a letter or decorative note to their person telling them why they are grateful to have them in their life. Process the activity by asking students to share some different ways that they could hand deliver their note or share it with their friend/family member in person.

Option 3: Gratitude Walk

Taking a walk and getting some fresh air is something to be grateful for in itself! But, take it one step further with this targeted gratitude walk! Here are the walk instructions:

- Ask students what kinds of things they are grateful for in nature.
- Give each student a clipboard with sticky note and a pencil.
- Lead them on a 10-20 minute walk outside and around the school building.
- On their sticky note or note card, have them write or draw at least 3 things they are grateful for that they see or experience on their walk.
- After the walk, display all sticky notes or notecards; let students do a Gallery Walk to read the displayed note cards.

Academic Success Strategy: Organizing Your Backpack

<u>Counselor Directions</u>: Students need to know that a well-organized backpack is their main tool for doing well in school! Today's academic strategy will help them to keep this main tool organized for easy and efficient use. Below are the steps to help them clean and organize their backpack for optimal use.

Steps

1. Hand out the following backpack organization checklist and read it together as a class.
2. Model how to use the checklist to organize a sample backpack.
3. Next, have students pair up in order to help each other organize their backpacks.
4. Give the pairs some time to clean out their backpack according to the checklist and then check off the item on the checklist; partners should especially make sure that their other half has actually done all that is checked off their checklist.
5. Remind students to clean out/organize their backpack weekly and encourage them to take an extra backpack checklist or 2 to use the next time they organize it on their own.
6. Finally, remind students that they can also fill in a request to organize their backpack in the counselor's office.

If you have any students that cannot complete the backpack organization in this twenty-minute period, consider working with them in a group setting the following day to finish the job.

Academic Success Strategy:
Backpack Organization Checklist

Student Directions: Review each step below to organize your backpack. Then check off the step as you do each one for your backpack cleanout. Happy Organizing!

My back pack is well-organized when it has:

- ☐ **My name written on the backpack in permanent marker**
- ☐ **No major rips or graffiti**
- ☐ **Workable zipper(s)**
- ☐ **No loose papers (all papers are secured in their binder or folder)**
- ☐ **A binder and homework folders with completed schoolwork inside**
- ☐ **A pen and pencil inside**
- ☐ **Fewer than five recreational items inside (toys, food, novels, etc.)**

Conflict Resolution at Family Events

Counselor Directions: In starting this activity, carefully explain that this class discussion is for exploring minor conflicts; tell students that conversations about major family conflicts (violence, substance abuse, etc.) should be had privately between the counselor and student.

Steps

1. Brainstorm with students the type of **minor** family conflicts that can occur during a holiday meal such as Thanksgiving.
2. Ask students, "How might a student with strong conflict resolution skills help their family if an interpersonal problem occurs during Thanksgiving?"
3. Show the conflict resolution poster, review the poster steps and how to fill out a counselor request form to get adult help, especially if someone is begin bullied.
4. Ask a few volunteers to try acting out each of the conflict resolution steps while you "bother" them with a common minor family conflict that can occur during Thanksgiving such as:
   - not wanting to have to do all the dishes alone
   - someone taking too much dessert so there's none for you
   - a family member not liking a gift they are given
5. After the role play, process the activity with a few guiding questions such as:
   - What went well in this role play?
   - What are some other ways you might resolve this type of family conflict?
   - What types of family conflicts should you NEVER get involved in and always seek adult help for? *(answer: major ones, especially if there is an unsafe situation occurring)*

Crucial Reminder for Students:
Be sure to remind students that they should never get involved in the family conflict with conflict resolution steps 2 or 3 if they feel that the conflict is getting unsafe or violent. In those cases, it is crucial to go straight to step 4 and enlist the help of a trusted adult.

December's Theme:
Building Hope & Friendship

Note to Counselor
While the 2020 social justice protests shined a direct spotlight on righting systemic inequities and racism within our society, the American School Counselor Association (2019) has long advocated for social justice. Accordingly, social justice themes of celebrating differences and raising each other up are woven into every lesson of this book (e.g., October's lesson on supporting and accepting those with mental health issues, January's lesson on connecting with others by looking for commonalities, etc.). However, December's themes of hope and friendship especially highlight these ideas. I encourage you to use the following books, discussion questions, hope building strategies, and talk show activities to shine your own light on supporting students in social justice.

American School Counselor Association Standards Alignment
Mindsets
M1. Belief in development of whole self, including a healthy balance of mental, social/emotional and physical well-being
Behaviors
B-SMS 9. Demonstrate personal safety skills
B-SS 5. Demonstrate ethical decision-making and social responsibility
B-LS 3. Use time-management, organizational and study skills

Objectives
The student will:
- Explore hope as a mental health support strategy.
- Practice strategies to keep their notebook neat and organized each week.
- Define emergencies and identify how to get help in an emergency situation.
- Apply the four steps of peaceful conflict resolution to conflicts specific to this season.

Materials
- Notebook Organization Checklist, chart paper, markers, *A Flicker of Hope* by Julia Cook or some other hope-themed picture book (if you'd like to add a bibliocounseling element to this lesson), paper, pencils

- Printables from August's Lesson: Do You Have an Emergency? posterette, Request to See the Counselor forms/instructions, conflict resolution posterette

Lesson Steps
DAY ONE

1. Introduction (5 min): Re-introduce yourself by stating your name and your role in the school. Review how students can fill out a Request to See the Counselor form in order to meet with you to talk about any problem they are having, use the attached request forms/instructions if necessary. Show the Do You Have an Emergency? poster to review what defines an emergency. Tell students that they should tell you or another adult immediately if they have an emergency and that they don't need to fill out a request form for emergencies. Remind students that all school staff must report "3 hurts" emergencies to another adult (parent, counselor, assistant principal, etc.) in order to keep students safe.

2. Opening Activity (5 min): Ask students what things make them feel hopeful and hopeless during holiday time.

3. Bibliocounseling (15 min): If you'd like to add a bibliocounseling element to this lesson, read aloud *A Flicker of Hope* by Julia Cook or some other picture book with themes of hope, acceptance, and/or asking for help (see attached book list with activity ideas). Begin by showing the picture book to the class and asking students to guess what it might be about. Read the book aloud to the class. Discuss the main theme of the story with the class as it relates to being a hope builder, how hope can help us to right injustices in the world, and how we all need hope to get through tough times.

4. Mental Health Support Strategy- Hope Building (10 min): Have the class generate a list of things we can all do to build hope in others if they ask us for help during a tough time or even if we want to offer help because we see them struggling. Write the class list on chart paper- see attached example list for ideas. Through discussion, guide them to the idea that when we help others, it naturally builds up our own feelings of self-worth while helping another person (discussion questions attached).

5. Conflict Resolution Practice (10 min): Briefly discuss with students that conflicts can be common at this time of year since both students and adults are excited about the upcoming break and also tired from all the schoolwork they've done so far. Show the conflict resolution posterette, review the poster steps and how to fill out a counselor request form if they need help or if someone is bullying. Ask students to give some typical conflicts that come up for students at this time of year. Then, have a few volunteers act out each of the conflict resolution steps while you "bother" them with a student-suggested conflict. After the role play, process the activity with a few guiding questions such as:
   - What went well in this role play?

- What are some other ways you might resolve this type of conflict?
- What types of conflicts should you seek adult help for immediately?

6. Closure (5 min): Wrap up the lesson by asking students to share their opinions of the following question with a partner: What was the most important thing you learned today?

7. Informal Lesson Evaluation (5 min): End the lesson with a thumbs up-thumbs down evaluation with the class. Have students show a thumbs up or thumbs down as you read them each of the following evaluation statements:
   - I understood this lesson.
   - I enjoyed this lesson.
   - I know how to help someone who feels hopeless.

DAY TWO

1. Introduction (5 min): Re-introduce yourself by stating your name and your role in the school. Review how students can fill out a Request to See the Counselor form in order to meet with you to talk about any problem they are having, use the attached request forms/instructions if necessary. Show the Do You Have an Emergency? poster to review what defines an emergency. Tell students that they should tell you or another adult immediately if they have an emergency and that they don't need to fill out a request form for emergencies. Remind students that all school staff must report "3 hurts" emergencies to another adult (parent, counselor, assistant principal, etc.) in order to keep students safe.

2. Opening Activity (5 min): Ask the class how we can use the ideas that they generated on chart paper (in Day One of this lesson) to create a hope building community in their own school.

3. Connection to Day One Activity- Talk Show (20 min): Tell students that they will use a talk show format to discuss the hope building ideas that were written on the chart paper in Day One of this lesson. Follow the steps in the attached Talk Show description.

4. Academic Success Strategy- Organize your Notebook (20 min): Briefly discuss with students that a well-organized notebook is another important tool for doing well in school. Use the attached Organize Your Notebook steps and checklist to guide them in today's academic strategy.

5. Closure (5 min): Wrap up the lesson by asking students what they are going to be most hopeful for during the next school break. Allow them to share their answers with the class.

6. Lesson Evaluation (5 min): End the lesson with a thumbs up-thumbs down evaluation with the class. Have students show their thumbs as you read them each of the following evaluation statements:
   - I understood this lesson.
   - I enjoyed this lesson.
   - I know the steps to keeping my notebook well-organized.

Bibliocounseling Book List & Activities

<u>Counselor Information</u>: Bibliocounseling is the practice of using of books, or other media, to teach social-emotional skills, such as conflict resolution (ASCA, 2019). This form of counseling is an effective intervention to use with all ages of students! Sometimes, I meet skeptical high school counselors who don't believe this practice will work with the older kids who are transitioning into adulthood...to which I always reply that the billion-dollar audio book industry proves otherwise. Our brains are even hardwired for storytelling. Humans have evolved over millions of years of storytelling, so the sound of the human voice reading a story is a naturally soothing and instinctual way for a person of any age to learn (Lerner, 2019). Below are several excellent title suggestions for picture books that include themes of home, acceptance, friendship, and celebrating diversity. I've also included some examples of thought-provoking comprehension questions in case you have extra time with your class and would like to build literacy skills during guidance lessons. In addition, there are some other ways to actively involve students during read aloud time at the bottom of this page.

Possible Read Aloud Titles:
- *The Storyteller's Candle* by Lucia Gonzalez and Lulu Delacre
- *My Diary from Here to There* by Amada Irma Perez
- *Flicker of Hope* by Julia Cook
- *Sulwe,* by Lupita Nyongo
- *Katie Loves the Kittens* by John Himmelman
- *Separate is Never Equal* by Duncan Tomatium
- *Lights for Gita* by Rachna Gilmore (and other Gita books by Rachna Gilmore)
- *Grandfather's Journey* by Allen Say
- *The Color of Home* by Mary Hoffman
- *The Have A Good Day Cafe* by Frances Park

Examples of Discussion/Comprehension Questions:
- Are there examples of justice or injustice in the story? Explain.
- What is the problem in the book?
- What is the solution?
- How is this similar to a problem or solution you have in your life?
- What did you learn from the book?
- Would you recommend this book to someone else? Why or why not?

Ways to Actively Involve Students in Read Aloud Time
- Have students tell their partner what just happened in the story.
- Have students tell their partner who has power in the story and how this makes them feel. Is it fair or unfair?
- Have pairs act out the story to each other as the teacher reads aloud.
- At the end of the read aloud time, have students close their eyes and imagine the next part of the story.

Mental Health Support Strategy: Hope Building

Counselor Information: Building hope for ourselves and sharing or inspiring hope in others is a major protective factor against mental health struggles such as ruminating thoughts, despair, resentment, etc. For this reason, it is important that we identify hope building as a strategy with our students and teach them how to create and use this skill! Begin this activity by having the class generate a list of things we can all do to build hope in others if they ask us for help during a tough time or even if we want to offer help because we see them struggling. Write the class list on chart paper; an example list is below.

Hope Building Activities
- Listen as your friend vents- Tell them, "I see you, I hear you, I'm listening".
- Tell a trusted adult if someone seems hopeless.
- Give a tissue and a hug if someone needs to cry.
- Help a family member with their chores or homework if they feel overwhelmed.
- Invite them to take a walk with you and your pet.
- Play a sport with them.
- Read a hopeful story to them.
- Ask how you can help.
- Make a positive plan for solving the problem.
- Brainstorm ideas for how to help with your parents.
- Share a chocolate bar with them.

Discussion
Wrap up the activity with a short discussion on the following topics/questions:
- How can building hope in others serve as a mental health support strategy?
- How can building hope in others prevent student crises?
- How can building hope in others lead to more equal and equitable conditions for all people?
- When we help others, it naturally builds up our own feelings of self-worth while helping another person. Why do you think this happens?
- Why is it important to help people with a problem or hopelessness before their problem gets to crisis mode?

Finally, let students know that they will do a follow-up application activity on this topic in the next guidance lesson.

Talk Show

<u>Counselor Directions</u>: Follow the steps below to lead student in the energizing and insightful activity, Talk Show; it allows them to explore the hope building process in a totally different medium- the talk show!

Steps:
1. Introduce the activity by telling students that they will use a talk show format to discuss the hope building ideas that were written on the chart paper in Day One of this lesson.
2. Organize the class into table groups and have them pick an idea from the chart paper list and then write 3-5 questions and answers about how to carry out the idea.
3. Give groups time to practice their "talk shows"- about 5-15 minutes.
4. Then each group can perform their show to the class.

**Be sure to briefly model the Q&A creation/practice/presentation first.
Modeling Example- Call up a few students to model the hope building activity, "listen while your friend vents" or "make a plan" with you in the talk show format. Begin by assigning each student a role (director, Q&A writer, talk show host, talk show expert guest, etc.); then show the class how you all work together to generate questions/answers which the writer could take notes on. Next, model how the host and guest could act out the Q&A under the guidance of the director- such as:

➢ Host: *What should someone do if their friend is feeling hopeless over injustice towards people of color?*
➢ Expert Guest- *Well, in my studies of hope at Harvard, we found that people feel less hopeless when they vent to a friend or make a plan for positive change.*
➢ Host: *What is venting?*
➢ EG: *Venting is when someone talks about a problem situation just to "get it off their chest".*
➢ Host: *And how could someone make a plan to positively change this injustice?*
➢ EG: *Well, there are as many plans as people are creative! Which means tons! For example, a student could make a plan to write and film a YouTube video on things kids/teens can do to promote justice for all people, such as a marching alongside their parents in peaceful protests against racism.*

*Extension Project: Consider enlisting the help of other staff in your school to videotape and broadcast these "Talk Shows" to the entire student body- that way everyone learns how to be a hope builder. This will further the mission of creating a school-wide hope building community. Be sure to work with your principal on this task, as it will require admin and parent approval.

Academic Success Strategy: Organize your Notebook

<u>Counselor Information</u>: A well-organized notebook is another important tool for doing well in school. As we all know, a 3-ring notebook with subject-labeled section dividers (or some organizational equivalent) is crucial for school success so that students have a place to keep all schoolwork papers neat and organized by subject. For this reason, the academic strategy today is to teach students the importance of organizing their notebook regularly. Let's jump into some steps for how to do this.

Steps:
1. Briefly discuss with students that a well-organized notebook is another important tool for doing well in school. Explain to the class that a 3-ring notebook with subject-labeled section dividers is crucial for school success so that they have a place to keep all papers neat and organized by subject.
2. Tell them that their academic strategy today is to organize their notebook regularly and you will show them an efficient and easy way to do it!
3. Hand out the following notebook organization checklist and read it together.
4. Model how to use the checklist to organize a sample notebook while the class watches you.
5. Direct each student to work with a partner so that they can help each other organize their notebook. Students should carefully double check that their partner has actually done what they checked off on the checklist.
6. Give students some time to set up or organize their notebook according to the checklist, checking off the items on the checklist as they work.
7. Remind students to clean out/organize their notebook weekly and encourage them to take an extra notebook checklist to use at home; alternately, they can fill in a request to organize their backpack in the counselor's office.

   If you have any students that cannot complete the notebook organization in this twenty-minute period, consider working with them in a group setting the following day to finish the job.

Note About Working with Young Students:
You may want to skip the notebook organization if you work with very young children or if your students are encouraged to use something other than a notebook. In that case, you might just proceed to the following discussion questions or substitute a different organizational tool (such as a system of folders) if your students/school do not use notebooks.

Notebook Organization Checklist

Student Directions: Review each step below to organize your notebook. Then, check off the step as you do each one for your notebook cleanout. Happy Organizing!

My notebook is well-organized when it has:
- ☐ **My name on the front or inside cover of the notebook**
- ☐ **All papers secured in their correct subject section**
- ☐ **Completed work in every section**
- ☐ **No loose papers**
- ☐ **A homework folder with homework assignments inside**
- ☐ **Subject sections divided with labeled tabs**
- ☐ **A section for each subject**
- ☐ **No major rips, breaks, or graffiti**
- ☐ **Blank paper secured in a section(s)**

Discussion Questions
After you are done organizing your notebook, discuss the need to have materials for each class using the following questions/topics as a guide:
- Why is it important to have your materials for each class each day?
- Where should all these materials be kept? Why?
- Why do you think that not having school materials in class frustrates the disorganized individual? The teacher?
- How might not having all your materials get in the way of achieving school success?
- What school materials should students have with them in school every day? (Write their ideas in a materials list on chart paper to keep on display in the classroom).

January's Theme:
Blizzard! An Icebreaker Guidance Lesson

Counselor Information
While you can effectively use this lesson at any time of the school year, January is the perfect month for this snow-themed activity on building connections between students. Often, we start guidance lesson rotations with new classes at the start of the semester and new students frequently enroll at this time of year. This lesson serves as a fun icebreaker to build and strengthen bonds between students.

American School Counselor Association Standards Alignment
Mindsets
M 3. Sense of belonging in the school environment
Behaviors
B-LS 2. Demonstrate creativity
B-SS 2. Create positive and supportive relationships with other students
B-LS 4. Apply self-motivation and self-direction to learning

Objectives
The student will:
- Explore connecting with others as a mental health support strategy.
- Review (or introduce, if necessary) strategies to check and improve their grades each week.
- Define emergencies and identify how to get help in an emergency situation.
- Apply the four steps of peaceful conflict resolution to conflicts specific to this time of year.

Materials
- Notecards/tape OR 1 Saving Sam set of materials per group (a gummy worm, a gummy lifesaver, plastic cup, 2 paper clips), computer with grade software loaded or Weekly Grade Sheet template, paper, pencils, markers
- Printables from August Lesson: Do You Have an Emergency? posterette, Request to See the Counselor forms/instructions, conflict resolution posterette

Lesson Steps

DAY ONE

1. Introduction (5 min): Re-introduce yourself by stating your name and your role in the school. Review how students can fill out a Request to See the Counselor form in order to meet with you to talk about any problem they are having, use the attached request forms/instructions if necessary. Show the Do You Have an Emergency? poster to review what defines an emergency. Tell students that they should tell you or another adult immediately if they have an emergency and that they don't need to fill out a request form for emergencies. Remind students that all school staff must report "3 hurts" emergencies to another adult (parent, counselor, assistant principal, etc.) in order to keep students safe.

2. Opening Activity (5 min): Tell students that building connections and strengthening bonds between people are very important in life; as human beings, our brains are hard-wired to flourish when we interact with other people. Explain that today we will participate in an activity that can help us build connections with our classmates.

3. Mental Health Support Strategy- Connection with Others (20 min): Lead students in the icebreaker activity, Blizzard!, so they can experience the positive effects of building connections with others. The steps and discussion questions for this mental health support strategy are attached.

4. Conflict Resolution Practice (10 min): Briefly discuss with students that with strong interpersonal connections, also comes conflict- guide students to the idea that this is a normal and natural part of bonding with other people. Show the Conflict Resolution posterette, review the poster steps and how to fill out a counselor request form if someone needs help or is being bullied. Ask students what kinds of conflicts they are seeing at home and at school during this time of year (i.e., irritable parents over having to pay holiday or school supplies bills, friends being short with each other due to upcoming testing stress, new rumors starting now that everyone is back at school, etc.). Then, have a few volunteers act out each of the conflict resolution steps while you "bother" them with 1-2 of the above student-suggested conflicts. After the role play, process the activity with a few guiding questions such as:
   - What went well in this role play?
   - What are some other ways you might resolve this type of conflict?
   - Hold up a finger to show the number of your preferred step to handle conflicts; refer to the conflict resolution posterette to know which number goes with each step.

5. Closure (10 min): Wrap up the lesson by asking students to share their ideas about the following question with a partner: What other things could students do in a classroom to build connections and improve relationships with their classmates? Ask partners to share their ideas with the class.

6. Lesson Evaluation (5 min): End the lesson with a thumbs up-thumbs down evaluation with the class. Have students show a thumbs up or thumbs down as you read them each of the following evaluation statements:
    - I understood this lesson.
    - I enjoyed this lesson.
    - I know why it is important for people to connect with each other.

DAY TWO

1. Introduction (5 min): Re-introduce yourself by stating your name and your role in the school. Review how students can fill out a Request to See the Counselor form in order to meet with you to talk about any problem they are having, use the attached request forms/instructions if necessary. Show the Do You Have an Emergency? poster to review what defines an emergency. Tell students that they should tell you or another adult immediately if they have an emergency and that they don't need to fill out a request form for emergencies. Remind students that all school staff must report "3 hurts" emergencies to another adult (parent, counselor, assistant principal, etc.) in order to keep students safe.

2. Opening Activity (5 min): Ask the class how they could connect with a new person or friend. Tell the class that today you will teach them another connection activity so they are better able to bond with their classmates, and maybe even learn some things about a classmate they don't know well. Let them know that they will also do a grade check review as the academic success strategy.

3. Connection to Day One Activity- Icebreakers, Take Two! (20-30 min): Use the attached Icebreaker Take Two steps to lead the class through another opportunity to build interpersonal connections.

4. Academic Success Strategy (20 min): Review how to check their grades weekly; see attached Weekly Grade Checks if you haven't done this before with students and need the original set of activity steps. While reviewing, address these points with students:
    - Checking up on your grades at least once a week is one of the top strategies for academic success.
    - If you have trouble checking your grades weekly, fill out a Request to See the Counselor so we can help you.
    - Raise your hand if you have already checked your grades at least once during this semester.
    - Raise your hand if you need me to do a quick demo of how to do a weekly grades check, in order to refresh your memory.

If you work with young children who don't have weekly grades, you might skip #4 or introduce/review the importance of a home study spot with them. Then, have them draw, color, and present a picture of their home study spot; if they don't have a home study spot yet, they could design their ideal one in their illustration.

5. Closure (5 min): Wrap up the lesson by giving each student an index card to write or draw 1 thing they learned and one question they still have. Collect notecards to determine if any topics need to be re-taught in a future guidance lesson.

6. Lesson Evaluation (5 min): End the lesson with a thumbs up-thumbs down evaluation with the class. Have students show a thumbs up or thumbs down as you read them each of the following evaluation statements:
   - I understood this lesson.
   - I enjoyed this lesson.
   - Connecting with others can help improve my mental health.

Blizzard!

<u>Counselor Information</u>: Connecting with others is an important mental health support strategy. As humans, we are a social species and interaction with other people is not a luxury- it's a necessity for stable and healthy mental functioning! In this activity, students will have a chance to practice connecting with others and to reflect on how it makes them feel.

Blizzard Steps:

1. Hand out a piece of paper to each student and have them write 3 characteristics about themselves on the paper. No one should write their name on their paper.
2. Next have all the students circle up, crumple their paper into a ball, and throw it in the middle of the circle.
3. Tell each student to pick up a "snowball" that is not their own.
4. Have each student read their snowball aloud while the rest of the class tries to guess who wrote those 3 characteristics. You can have the writer step forward if no one can guess correctly.

Discussion

Once all students have read and/or "confessed" to their snowballs, have the class return to their seats. Foster a discussion about connectivity by using the following question prompts.

✓ What did you like or dislike about this ice breaker activity? Why?
✓ What common characteristics did you notice that multiple students wrote on their snowballs?
✓ Connecting with other people and finding things in common is really important. Why do you think this is important?
✓ How did this activity help to build connections between you and your classmates?
✓ How do you think connection with others can help prevent "3 Hurts" emergencies?

Icebreakers- Take Two!

<u>Counselor Directions</u>: Review the Day One icebreaker activity briefly by asking students how Blizzard! helped them to get to know each other a little better. Tell students that today they will continue building interpersonal connections and strengthening bonds by doing another icebreaker activity.

Steps to Facilitate Activity:
1. Choose one of the following icebreaker activities for the class to complete.
2. Review the activity instructions with the class.
3. Model the instructions so students understand exactly what to do.
4. Hand out materials and lead students through the activity.
5. Process the activity with the class using a few guiding discussion questions.

Discussion Questions (to follow the activity/s on the next page)
- What did you like best about this activity?
- What did you like least about this activity?
- How did it make you feel?
- In your opinion, did this activity foster connections in the class group? Why or why not?
- Is connecting with others a mental health support strategy- why or why not?

Icebreakers- Take Two! (Continued):
The Activities

Counselor Directions: Below are the Day Two activities that you can lead the class through. Choose the activity that is best suited to the age and interests of your student population (unless you have time to do both). Or you might even try letting the class choose their own activity!

Activity One- Famous Figures

Steps

1. Hand out notecards to each student and then have them write down the name of a famous athlete, actor, musician, or historical figure that has impacted them in a positive way.
2. Next, collect the notecards and have the class line up with their backs to you.
3. Go down the line of students, randomly taping one notecard to each student's back with the name of the famous person showing.
4. Now have students mingle around the room, trying to guess who is taped on their back by asking yes or no questions to their classmates- they can ask each classmate one yes/no question about the person on their back.
5. After 15 minutes, have students take their seat and write down who they think is on their back.
6. Finally let students take off and read the notecard on their back. Have each student share if they guessed correctly, who they originally wrote down on their first notecard, and why that person inspires them.

Activity Two-Saving Sam

Steps

1. Show the class the following materials: a gummy worm, a gummy lifesaver, a plastic cup, and two paper clips.
2. Tell students that they will be divided into groups and each group will get these materials to solve an imaginary rescue mission:

The gummy worm Sam was in his plastic cup-boat until it overturned in the ocean! His gummy lifesaver is under the boat and he is clinging to the top of the boat in the water so he doesn't drown. The mission is to help Sam put on the lifesaver jacket so he doesn't drown. But! The only tools you can use to help Sam are the paperclips and you can't touch anything with your hands.

3. Organize students into groups and give each group their gummy worm, lifesaver, cup, and 2 paperclips.
4. The first group to save Sam wins!

Weekly Grade Checks

Briefly discuss with students that doing well in school academically helps them to feel good about themselves, which, in turn, boosts their mental health. Remind the class that school counselors can help if students are failing or worried about classes/grades.
Tell students that today you will teach them an academic success strategy that will help them to boost their grades! If your students have access to a software or online program that tracks their grades, show them how to use this. For example, my school uses the computer system, Skyward, so I just demonstrate the software tutorial to show students how to access and review their grades and assignments. I show them how to interpret their weekly grade averages with all the assignments listed that contribute to that average. Alternately, if your school doesn't have a computerized grade system, you can create a Weekly Grade Sheet using the template below. Then, pass out and show students how to use the attached Weekly Grade Sheet to review their grades each week.

Weekly Grade Sheet for _____ **Date:** _____

Period and/or Subject:	Grade Average:	Comments (Reasons for Failing Average, if Applicable):	Teacher Signature:

ABC

February's Theme:
Are You Life Ready?

Counselor Note- The latest trend developing in the College and Career Readiness (CCR) movement is "Life Ready". This means that students graduate from high school with the ability to achieve their life goals because they have strong social and emotional learning skills. Here is a quote explaining more about this new trend from its founding organization, the School Superintendents' Association:

> *Being LIFE READY means students leave high school with the grit and perseverance to tackle and achieve their goals by demonstrating personal actualization skills of self-awareness, self-management, social-awareness, responsible decision making, and relationship skills. Students who are LIFE READY possess the growth mindset that empowers them to approach their future with confidence, to dream big and to achieve big. Our nation's schools provide social and emotional support and experiences to equip students with life skills to succeed in the present and in the future. While little research exists in the LIFE READY realm, AASA and the Redefining Ready! Campaign are currently studying how to best measure these life ready skills (AASA, 2018).*

American School Counselor Association Standards Alignment
Mindsets
M 6. Positive attitude toward work and learning
Behaviors
B-LS 9. Gather evidence and consider multiple perspectives to make informed decisions
B-SS 7. Use leadership and teamwork skills to work effectively in diverse teams

Objectives
The student will:
- Practice prioritizing tasks as a mental health support strategy.
- Define emergencies and identify how to get help in an emergency situation.
- Apply the four steps of peaceful conflict resolution to conflicts specific to this time of year.
- Identify the financial rewards of higher education.
- Discuss the concepts of being "life ready" and "college ready".

Materials
- List of Tasks for a Ten-Minute Period, timer, "Learn More, Earn More" infographic from Bigfuture.collegeboard.org, video clip of *You Can Go* or *5 Ways Ed Pays* from YouTube.com, internet with laptop or projector to show website infographic and YouTube video, markers and chart paper, pencils and scrap paper
- Printables from August Lesson: Do You Have an Emergency? posterette, Request to See the Counselor forms/instructions, conflict resolution posterette

Lesson Steps
DAY ONE

1. Introduction (5 min): Re-introduce yourself by stating your name and your role in the school. Review how students can fill out a Request to See the Counselor form in order to meet with you to talk about any problem they are having, use the attached request forms/instructions if necessary. Show the Do You Have an Emergency? poster to review what defines an emergency. Tell students that they should tell you or another adult immediately if they have an emergency and that they don't need to fill out a request form for emergencies. Remind students that all school staff must report "3 hurts" emergencies to another adult (parent, counselor, assistant principal, etc.) in order to keep students safe.

2. Opening Activity (10 min): Ask students to guess what being "life ready" might mean. Guide them to the "life ready" explanation in the Counselor Note at the beginning of this lesson. Next, explain to students that the goal of school is to prepare them to be successful in their adult college (define college with the class as ANY education after high school), career (including military if they choose it), and life experiences. Define the words *prioritize* and *efficient* with the class and then tell them that today we'll work on the "life ready" skills of self-management and decision-making through a prioritizing tasks activity. Also let the class know that in Day 2 of this lesson, we'll discuss being "college ready"; then in next month's lesson, we'll discuss being "career ready". (At this point, I will refer to these 3 terms without the quotes for the rest of the lesson plan since we have established them as set CCR terms.)

3. Mental Health Support Strategy- Prioritizing Tasks (30 min): Ask students how they feel when they have too much homework, or too many home chores to do in a short time period. Guide them to the idea that having too many tasks in a short time period can cause some people to feel stressed. Explain that today they will learn about prioritizing tasks which helps to lessen stress when there is too much to do. Follow the steps in the attached Prioritizing Tasks Activity to lead students through this mental health support strategy.

4. Conflict Resolution Practice (10 min): Lead students in a brief review and role play of the Four Steps of Conflict Resolution by following these steps:
   - ✓ Show the Conflict Resolution Poster.

✓ Review the poster steps and how to fill out a counselor request form if you need help or if someone is bullying you.
✓ Ask one student volunteer to act out each of the conflict resolution steps while you "bother" them with an annoying behavior like kicking their chair or tapping your pencil loudly.
✓ After the role play, process the activity with this question: What are some other ways you might resolve this type of conflict?

5. Closure (5 min): Wrap up the lesson by asking students EITHER to explain how prioritizing activities and managing time well leads to positive mental health –OR- to share which activities from the list they enjoyed doing the most.

6. Lesson Evaluation (5 min): Have students do a thumbs up-thumbs down lesson evaluation with you while you read them each of the following evaluation statements:
   • I understood this lesson.
   • I know what "life ready" means.
   • I enjoyed this lesson.

DAY TWO

1. Introduction (5 min): Re-introduce yourself by stating your name and your role in the school. Review how students can fill out a Request to See the Counselor form in order to meet with you to talk about any problem they are having, use the attached request forms/instructions if necessary. Show the Do You Have an Emergency? poster to review what defines an emergency. Tell students that they should tell you or another adult immediately if they have an emergency and that they don't need to fill out a request form for emergencies. Remind students that all school staff must report "3 hurts" emergencies to another adult (parent, counselor, assistant principal, etc.) in order to keep students safe.

2. Opening Activity (10 min): Hand out scrap paper and ask students to write down the most important thing they learned in the last lesson about CCR and being "Life Ready" (if a lot of time has gone by between Day One and Day Two of this guidance lesson, then you may need to review the main points that you covered in Day One). Introduce today's topic by telling the class that they will learn about being "college ready"; define the term "college readiness" for the class or group. Next, discuss college and higher education as ANY schooling or training after high school (post-secondary education) such as a mechanic training institute, a two-year community college, a four-year university, etc. Explain to students that higher education is an important topic for them because it lets them earn more money!

3. Connection to Day One Activity- Finances and College (15 min): Discuss that one of the ways to be life ready is to have a plan for "good earning power". Discuss what this term means, how college can help with this, and how everyone can go! Next show students one or both of the following video clips to introduce to them the

importance of higher education as a means to increase their earning power. After the video/s, ask a few students to summarize the video. Then ask the class to tell you what they learned from the video and where they would go to get more info on colleges.

- *Five Ways Ed Pays*: you can find it at https://www.YouTube.com/watch?v=spNDLD2KRuA
- *You Can Go to College* from Cbyoucango: you can find it at https://www.YouTube.com/watch?v=3J7AvMFifR8

4. Academic Success Strategy- "Learn More, Earn More" Activity (15 min): Show and facilitate a class discussion about the infographic "Learn More, Earn More" at https://bigfuture.collegeboard.org/get-started/know-yourself/learn-more-earn-more. Follow the steps in the attached "Learn More, Earn More" sheet to explore this idea as an academic success strategy.

5. Closure (5 min): Wrap up the lesson by asking students to draw a quick picture or doodle of the most important college ready idea that they learned today. If needed, you can display the pictures as an opener to the next lesson about being career ready.

6. Lesson Evaluation (5 min): End the lesson with a thumbs up-thumbs down evaluation with the class. Have students show a thumbs up or thumbs down as you read them each of the following evaluation statements:
- I understood this lesson.
- I enjoyed this lesson.
- I know how to get more information on going to and paying for college.

Prioritizing Tasks Activity

<u>Counselor Directions</u>: Prioritizing tasks is an important mental health support strategy for students to learn because this skill significantly reduces stress during busy times. Begin the activity with the following introductory steps.

Introduction to Activity
- Ask the class how they feel when they have too much homework, or too many home chores to do in a short time period.
- Guide them to the idea that having too many tasks in a short time period can cause some people to feel stressed.
- Have students tell a partner what happens when they feel stressed and then share out with the class.
- Explain that today they will learn about prioritizing tasks which helps to lessen stress when there is too much to do.
- Review the words *prioritize* and *efficient* with the class and then tell them to apply these words as they do the following activity.

Prioritizing Tasks Activity (Continued)

Activity Steps

1. Show students the attached List of Tasks for a Ten-Minute Period.
2. Read over the list with them and explain that all of these tasks together actually take an hour or more (not 10 minutes) to complete.
3. Tell students that they will now work in groups to decide on and then act out as many tasks as possible in a 10-minute period in order to earn the most points that they can.
4. Tell them that once you start the 10-minute timer, they must work together in their group to:
   - ✓ choose their group tasks
   - ✓ complete chosen tasks
   - ✓ add up their points for all the tasks they did before the time goes off
5. Make sure to first model the checked group actions above with a few student volunteers so everyone understands how to do this activity.
6. Divide the class into groups, set the timer for 10 minutes and tell students to "Go!"
7. After the 10-minute period is up, award a prize to the group with the most points and then use the following questions to process the activity with the class.

Discussion Questions

- How did you feel as you completed this activity?
- Do you feel your group managed their time well (in an efficient way)? Why or why not?
- Think about some of the decisions that your group made. Why did you make these decisions?
- How did your group decide on the value of each task?
- Was communication important in this activity? In life? Why or why not?
- How did you prioritize your list into which tasks to do first? Or not at all?
- Was your group efficient overall? Why or why not?
- How does practicing an activity like this make you "life ready"?

Alternate Activity

If you work with very young students or if you are short on time, you can simplify this activity by:
   - ➢ decreasing the List of Tasks (attached) to just 2-4
   - ➢ decreasing the discussion questions (above) to just 2-4
   - ➢ removing the most difficult tasks and questions

List of Tasks for Ten-Minute Period

❖ **Have everyone in the group draw a tree on a piece of paper and color it. (15 points)**

❖ **Give every group member a (nice!) nickname. (15 points)**

❖ **Have one group member read a paragraph in a book to the rest of the group members. (15 points)**

❖ **Have everyone in the group crawl under 3 desks. (10 points)**

❖ **Sit down in a chair, then stand up- repeat 20 times. (5 points)**

❖ **Have everyone in the class sign their name to one piece of paper. (20 points)**

❖ **Have the group make a conga line and conga dance from one side of the classroom to the other. (10 points, 5 bonus points for each non-group member you can get to join your conga line)**

❖ **Have every group member make a different animal sound. (10 points)**

❖ **Blindfold one group member and lead them safely from one side of the classroom to the other. (5 points)**

❖ **Ask the teacher one question. (5 points)**

Learn More, Earn More

<u>Counselor Directions</u>: Another important part of being "Life Ready" is understanding that increased learning and knowledge is very likely to increase earning potential in life! Explain to the class that this is one of the reasons that it pays to be a lifelong learner. Introduce this concept as an academic success strategy by showing the following College Board infographic and following the activity steps below.

Steps
1. Show students the infographic "Learn more, Earn More" at https://bigfuture.collegeboard.org/get-started/know-yourself/learn-more-earn-more.
2. Explain each of the kinds of degrees listed in the infographic and the salary associated with each degree.
3. Guide the class in a discussion about the infographic by writing the following discussion questions on the board or chart paper.
4. While you write, give students a few minutes to use the Think-Pair-Share activity to generate some answers to the following questions.

Discussion Questions
*   Thumbs up/down if you've considered attending a university, technical/trade school or community college.
*   What is the financial advantage of attending college?
*   Have you ever talked with your parent/guardian about how much money you want to make at your future job? (More advanced version of this question: Have you talked with your family about how much money you might earn with the degree you need for the job you want?) If so, how did this conversation go? If not, how might you start this conversation?
*   Why do you think planning for college now is an academic success strategy?
*   How will the academic success strategies you are learning in guidance lessons (organizing your backpack, checking your grades weekly, etc.) help you get to college? How will these strategies help you to be college ready?
*   Where could you find information about the earning power of the type of degree you would like to pursue?
*   What is a professional degree and why do you think it can earn someone so much money?

Alternate Activity
If you work with young students or if you are short on time, you can simplify this activity by decreasing the number of questions to just 2-4, removing the most difficult ones.

March's Theme:
Are You Career Ready?

American School Counselor Association Standards Alignment
Mindsets
M 4. Understanding that postsecondary education and lifelong learning are necessary for long term career success
Behaviors
B-LS 5. Apply media and technology skills
B-LS 7. Identify long- and short-term academic, career and social/ emotional goals
B-SMS 7. Demonstrate effective coping skills when faced with a problem

Objectives
The student will:
- Practice three stress reducers as a mental health support strategy.
- Define emergencies and identify how to get help in an emergency situation.
- Apply the four steps of peaceful conflict resolution to conflicts involving rumors.
- Use the O'net website to identify preferred career options.
- Discuss the concept of being "career ready".

Materials
- Hand Model of the Brain handout, laptops or tablets for students to use with internet connection, bingo boards, bingo chips, video clip of *9 Highest Paying Jobs Without a [4 Year] College Degree* from YouTube.com (https://youtu.be/NcKXxJ0XdAI), internet with laptop or projector to show the YouTube video, O'net website, previously made college ready doodles -OR- pencils and scrap paper
- Printables from August Lesson: Do You Have an Emergency? posterette, Request to See the Counselor forms/instructions, Four Steps of Conflict Resolution posterette

Lesson Steps
DAY ONE

1. Introduction (5 min): Re-introduce yourself by stating your name and your role in the school. Review how students can fill out a Request to See the Counselor form in order to meet with you to talk about any problem they are having, use the attached request forms/instructions if necessary. Show the Do You Have an Emergency? poster to review what defines an emergency. Tell students that they should tell you or another adult immediately if they have an emergency and that they don't need to fill out a request form for emergencies. Remind students that all school staff must report "3 hurts" emergencies to another adult (parent, counselor, assistant principal, etc.) in order to keep students safe.

2. Opening Activity (10 min): Ask students to do a quick art walk to look over the closure doodle drawings that the class made at the end of the last lesson to show the most important thing they learned about being "college ready". Now ask students what being "career ready" might mean and how it relates to being "college ready".
   If you didn't do the last College & Career Readiness (CCR) lesson with this class, instead have them do a quick doodle drawing of what they think "career ready" means; then do the above art walk and briefly discuss it.
   Guide them to the idea that a "career ready" student is one that is ready to successfully complete the next step after high school on the road to their desired career. Tell them that today's lesson will explore how to be "career ready". (At this point, I will refer to this term without the quotes for the rest of the lesson plan since we have established it as a set CCR term.)

3. Career Ready Activity (20 min): Discuss that one of the ways to be career ready is to think about how much training they will need after high school for their future career. Discuss that this doesn't always mean attending a university and that some careers require a different type of training after high school. If your students are old enough to conceptualize the following terms, define and discuss the "earning potential" (how much money one can potentially earn from a certain job) and "job growth outlook" (how many of these types of jobs will be available in the future). Next, show students the YouTube video clip called 9 Highest Paying Jobs Without a [4 Year] College Degree https://youtu.be/NcKXxJ0XdAI to introduce them to the types of careers that: don't require a 4 year university degree, do have good earning potential (you may need to review or simplify this term), and are projected to offer lots of jobs in the future. After showing the video/s, ask a few students to summarize the video. Then ask the class to tell you what they learned from the video.
   If your students are too young for this topic, you can instead show them this Sesame Street career video with Justice Sonia Sotomayor and discuss its main points after viewing: https://www.YouTube.com/watch?v=EHICz5MYxNQ.

4. Conflict Resolution Practice- Rumor Role Play (10 min): Lead students in a brief review and role play of the Four Steps of Conflict Resolution by following these steps:
   a. Review the poster steps and how to fill out a counselor request form if student needs help or is bulled.
   b. Discuss with the class how rumors are annoying and make most of us mad if we are the target.
   c. Ask one student volunteer to act out the four steps while counselor "bothers" them by pretending to spread rumors about them.
   d. After the role play, process the activity with this question: What main step would you use to solve a rumor problem (show the step with your finger number)? What are some other ways you might resolve this type of conflict?

5. Closure (10 min): Wrap up the lesson by asking students to tell a partner what kind of training they think they might need after high school to prepare for their future career. Share out responses with the class.

6. Lesson Evaluation (5 min): Have students do a thumbs up-thumbs down lesson evaluation with you while you read them each of the following evaluation statements:
   - I understood this lesson.
   - I can name some careers that have good earning potential and good job growth outlook.
   - I enjoyed this lesson.

DAY TWO

1. Introduction (5 min): Re-introduce yourself by stating your name and your role in the school. Review how students can fill out a Request to See the Counselor form in order to meet with you to talk about any problem they are having, use the attached request forms/instructions if necessary. Show the Do You Have an Emergency? poster to review what defines an emergency. Tell students that they should tell you or another adult immediately if they have an emergency and that they don't need to fill out a request form for emergencies. Remind students that all school staff must report "3 hurts" emergencies to another adult (parent, counselor, assistant principal, etc.) in order to keep students safe.

2. Opening Activity (5 min): Have students get into pairs. In silence, each partner should pantomime a career they are most interested in having when they finish school (or if your students are very young, you might phrase this as "what they want to be when they grow up"). After each partner has a chance to act out their preferred career, ask for 2-3 volunteers to tell what career their partner acted out.

3. Connection to Day One Activity- Exploring Careers with O'net (15 min): Now that the class has discussed some different careers in the Day One activity, briefly show them around the O'net website so they can explore some other careers that they are

interested in. After you show them how to navigate around the site, tell students to spend 10-15 minutes exploring the careers on O'net that most interest them as future occupations: www.onetonline.org/find/.

4. Mental Health Support Strategy- Stress Reducers (15 min): Ask students why someone might feel stressed over discussing their college or career future after high school. Ask students to stand if the upcoming testing season makes them feel stressed out or worried. Have students sit down again and tell them you will be giving them info and teaching them a calming strategy to help them if they feel stressed or worried. Lead students through the following steps:
   - Using the Hand Model of the Brain attachment, show students how to use their own hand to make a model of their brain- explain what happens when they are stressed and the hand-brain model "flips its lid".
   - Ask students how to "close the lid"- guide them to the idea that stress management strategies allow them to fold their fingers back over their palm or establish connection again between upper and lower brain parts.
   - Teach them 3 fast stress management strategies that "close the lid":
     - ✓ Hand/arm self-massage- have students use their right hand to massage their left palm or arm, then switch to left hand massaging right palm or arm.
     - ✓ Self-hug- have students wrap their arms around themselves; explain to students that with this "self-hug", we give ourselves *contact comfort. *This means that through touch, we increase feelings of safety and reduce the nervous system's reactivity to pain and threat.*
     - ✓ Finger mustache- have students curl their forefinger in an upside-down "U" and place it under their nose around their upper lip, have them inhale through nose/exhale through mouth 5 times while holding this position; explain to the class that their finger mustache applies a calming hold on this lip-nose area pressure point.
   - Process the activity with these questions: How are the 3 above techniques mental health support strategies? What else can you do to calm your stress and anger once you've "flipped your lid"? How can this help to prevent a 3 hurts emergency?

5. Academic Success Strategy- Advanced School Success Bingo (15 min): Play the advanced version of the School Success Bingo game to review the academic success strategies they have learned. Hand out the bingo cards that students made in a previous guidance lesson and follow the attached game steps.
   If you haven't played the original School Success Bingo in a previous lesson, use the original bingo materials/steps from the August lesson and then play the original version instead of this lesson's advanced version.

6. Closure (5 min): Wrap up the lesson by asking students to tell a partner their favorite way to "close their lid".

7. Lesson Evaluation (5 min): End the lesson with a thumbs up-thumbs down evaluation with the class. Have students show a thumbs up or thumbs down as you read them each of the following evaluation statements:
   - I understood this lesson.
   - I enjoyed this lesson.
   - I know at least 3 ways to calm myself if I am feeling stressed.
   - I found one or more careers I am interested in on the O'net website.

Hand Model of the Brain: Don't Flip Your Lid!

<u>Student Information</u>: When our brain is calm and working well, it is like the closed fist below, where all parts are connected and working well together.

	In this hand-brain model, your lower/mid brain is made up of: your wrist/spinal cord, your palm/brain stem and your thumb/limbic region; your thumb is where your big emotions (example- fight or flight) exist. Your upper brain is made up of your folded fingers/cortex where your higher-level thinking and learning occur- which is what you are using right now in this lesson!
	However, when you get very stressed or angry, your upper and lower brain disconnect so your brain can focus all of its energy on the mid/lower brain's fight or flight response. When this stress response happens, it's like our fingers fly open because the upper brain is no longer connected to the lower brain; this means our upper brain is not working and thinking clearly. Some people call this "flipping your lid!"

Advanced School Success Bingo

Counselor Directions:

- Call out a bingo letter and success strategy.
- If a student has that combination of bingo letter and strategy, they must raise their hand.
- When you call on the student/s raising their hand/s, they must either:
    - explain the strategy if it starts with a letter from A-L.
      -OR-
    - tell of a time they have used or will use the strategy in their own life if it starts with a letter from M-Z.

      So, for example, if you call out "B-goals", and a student raises their hand because they have this combination, they would have to explain the goals success strategy before earning a bingo chip from you (since goals starts with "g" which is in the A-L range, requiring them to explain the strategy).
- If the student is able to do this, give them a bingo chip to place in the correct spot on the bingo card. If not, they don't earn the bingo chip.
- The first group member to get five chips placed in a row or column calls out "BINGO" and wins a prize. After someone wins, have group members clear their cards of game pieces and start again.
- Collect the bingo cards after the game to be handed out again for a future game.

April's Theme:
Healthy Eating for Mental Health

American School Counselor Association Standards Alignment

Mindsets

M 1. Belief in development of whole self, including a healthy balance of mental, social/emotional and physical well-being

Behaviors

B-LS 3. Use time-management, organizational and study skills

B-SMS 9. Demonstrate personal safety skills

Objectives

The student will:

- Explore healthy eating as a mental health support strategy.
- Practice strategies to organize and use a planner each day.
- Define emergencies and identify how to get help in an emergency situation.
- Apply the four steps of peaceful conflict resolution to a bullying story.

Materials

- Printables from August Lesson: Do You Have an Emergency? posterette, Request to See the Counselor forms/instructions, conflict resolution posterette, bingo boards
- "Avoid Skipping Meals" video clip on YouTube https://www.YouTube.com/watch?v=DsXSXHurYCI, *Vicious* book by Hope Vanderberg *(or Bully Beans* by Julia Cook or HuffPost article listed below), planner checklists, sample planner, a planner for each student (prep ideas below if your students don't have or cannot buy their own planners), bingo chips, scrap paper and pencils

Lesson Steps
DAY ONE

1. Introduction (5 min): Re-introduce yourself by stating your name and your role in the school. Review how students can fill out a Request to See the Counselor form in order to meet with you to talk about any problem they are having, use the attached request forms/instructions if necessary. Show the Do You Have an Emergency?

poster to review what defines an emergency. Tell students that they should tell you or another adult immediately if they have an emergency and that they don't need to fill out a request form for emergencies. Remind students that all school staff must report "3 hurts" emergencies to another adult (parent, counselor, assistant principal, etc.) in order to keep students safe.

2. Opening Activity (5 min): Ask students to jot down or share with a family member their guess as to why healthy eating is important. Guide the class to the idea that healthy eating also affects mental health and why this is especially important when we are stressed by being homebound during a pandemic. Tell students that today they will watch a video clip to explore this idea.

3. Mental Health Support Strategy- Healthy Eating Habits (20 min): Tell students that the class will watch CNN's "Avoid Skipping Meals" with dietician Shayna Komar https://www.YouTube.com/watch?v=DsXSXHurYCI to learn about how healthy eating affects mental health. Follow the steps in the attached sheet called Healthy Eating Habits in order to guide students in exploring and processing this information.

4. Conflict Resolution Practice- Anti-Bullying Story (20 min): Lead students in an application of the Four Steps of Conflict Resolution to a story about bullying. Follow the steps in the attached activity called Anti-Bullying Story & Activity.

5. Closure (10 min): Wrap up the lesson by having students write a question that relates to something they learned today in this lesson. Collect for Day Two of this lesson.

6. Lesson Evaluation (5 min): Show the students the following statements and have them either respond with a thumbs up/down response to each question or jot down their answers with a simple "yes/no" and submit them to you.
   - I understood this lesson.
   - I know how healthy eating affects my mental health.
   - I enjoyed this lesson.

DAY TWO

1. Introduction (5 min): Re-introduce yourself by stating your name and your role in the school. Review how students can fill out a Request to See the Counselor form in order to meet with you to talk about any problem they are having, use the attached request forms/instructions if necessary. Show the Do You Have an Emergency? poster to review what defines an emergency. Tell students that they should tell you or another adult immediately if they have an emergency and that they don't need to fill out a request form for emergencies. Remind students that all school staff must report "3 hurts" emergencies to another adult (parent, counselor, assistant principal, etc.) in order to keep students safe.

2. Opening Activity: Connection to Day One Activity (10 min): Read the class some of the questions they wrote from the Day One Closure of this lesson. If possible, ask for volunteers to answer the question/s (alternately, you can just answer them yourself).

Tell students that today they will learn how to correctly use planners or agendas as an academic success strategy.

3. Academic Success Strategy- Use a Planner (30 min): Ask students to name some of the strategies they have learned for being successful in school. Tell the class that using a planner or agenda is another strategy for doing well in school. Briefly discuss that you will be teaching them how to use or improve upon their use of planners today! Follow the steps in the attached Using a Planner sheet to facilitate this academic success strategy with the class.

4. Closure (10 min): Wrap up the lesson by dividing the class into 5 groups, giving each group a planner checklist line item. Each group should work together to create a verbal explanation telling why their checklist item is the most important one for staying organized. Have each group present their explanation to the class for a fun and friendly competition. If this group work is not possible, have each student choose their favorite planner checklist line item and describe why it is the most important one for staying organized. They should submit their response to you.

5. Informal Lesson Evaluation (5 min): Show the students the following statements and have them either respond with a thumbs up/down response to each question or jot down their answers with a simple "yes/no" and submit them to you.
   - I understood this lesson.
   - I enjoyed this lesson.
   - I know how to use a planner to help me complete my school assignments.

🍎 Healthy Eating Habits 🍎

<u>Counselor Directions</u>: Ask the class why they think healthy eating is important. Tell students that they will learn from a registered dietician, Shayna Komar, about how healthy eating affects our mental health. Follow the steps below to guide students in this mental health support strategy!

Steps
1. Before showing the video, have students preview the following discussion questions (to be explored after watching the video clip) so they can think about these questions/topics as they are viewing CNN's "Avoid Skipping Meals".
2. Show the class the video clip with dietician Shayna Komar on YouTube at https://www.YouTube.com/watch?v=DsXSXHurYCI .
3. After the video, discuss each of the following questions.
   If you are in a distance learning environment, you can use your online platform such as Google Hangouts/Zoom or have students email you the answers to the questions. Alternately, they can discuss the questions with a family member and send you a brief writeup or video of their family discussion.

Video Discussion Questions (answers are also included in italics, but don't show them to the students):
- What happens to your body if you skip any meal? What happens if you aren't eating healthy? *It affects your blood sugar, mood, metabolism, and concentration.*
- Why do we need to eat every four hours? *To prevent our body starting starvation mode.*
- How is healthy eating a mental health support strategy? *If we eat healthy, our brains work better and we have better mental health functioning.*
- What might counselors or staff do if we learn that a student is eating unhealthily or skipping meals at school? *Talk to you, talk to the school nurse, make a plan for healthy eating with you, notify your parents/guardians.*

Alternate Video Activity
1. If you work with very young children, you can show them this alternate cartoon video about healthy eating from Kidshealth.org, *How the Body Works: Your Weight* at https://kidshealth.org/en/kids/healthy-weight-movie.html?WT.ac=ctg#catmovies
2. Foster a shorter, age-appropriate discussion of the video clip by decreasing the discussion questions above to just 1 or 2.

Anti-Bullying Story & Activity

Counselor Directions: Ask the class to share some ideas on what bullying is and how it causes problems for students; have them do this with a family member if they are distance learning. Follow the steps below to lead students in an application of the Four Steps of Conflict Resolution to a story about bullying/cyberbullying.

Steps

1. Review the following conflict resolution posterette steps and remind/show students how to fill out a counselor request form if they need help or experience bullying/cyberbullying.

2. Pick one of the short stories from the book *Vicious: True Stories by Teens about Bullying* and read all or just part of it aloud to the class.
   ➢ FYI- this book also has stories appropriate for upper elementary students.
   ➢ If you work with very young students, you might read *Bully Beans* by Julia Cook instead.
   ➢ If you don't have either book, you can find this HuffPost news story online and read just the beginning to young students or all of it to older students: "6-Year-Old Says No to Bullying with Sweet Back-To-School Shirt" at https://www.huffpost.com/entry/6-year-old-bullying-back-to-school-shirt_l_5d483e61e4b0aca341218094.

3. Ask the class: "What step on the conflict resolution posterette would you use to solve the problem in the story? Show the step's number with your finger or comment your number to me on our online platform."
   ➢ 1)Ignore.
   ➢ 2)Walk away.
   ➢ 3)Say an "I" message.
   ➢ 4)Tell an Adult.

4. If possible, have a few students explain why they picked their step and then give two students a bullying situation and let them apply the Four Steps of Conflict Resolution to this situation as they act it out in front of the class.

Academic Success Strategy: Using a Planner

<u>Counselor Directions</u>: Planners are an important tool for students to learn to use correctly! For this activity, each student in the class will need a planner or agenda book. If your students don't already have planners and cannot buy planners, you can make planners with the class! Doing so will probably require a second day for this activity, unless you have the students make their planners at home. Scatteredsquirrel.com has free planner downloadables that can be printed for students: https://scatteredsquirrel.com/printable/personal-planner/weekly-planner-printables/. If you use the Scattered Squirrel planners, you/students will need some time/materials to print the planner sheets and put them together (at least 1 class).

Planner Introduction Steps

Briefly discuss with students that using a planner or agenda is another strategy for doing well in school- here are some tips to cover in this discussion:

- Explain to the class that a student planner is a great tool for keeping track of what assignments to complete and when.
- Show them a sample planner that is organized by months or weeks.
- Demonstrate how to write down the assignments for completion next to each subject or class period.
- Model for students how to write down the due date and assignment, test, quiz, or project, as soon they enter the classroom or the teacher gives it (and what to do if the teacher gives no info on this).
- Show students how to cross off the completed assignments in order to keep track of which ones are left to do.

Planner Activity Steps

Now share the following planner checklist with the class. Be sure to model how to use the checklist with your sample planner.

- Have each student take out their planner or use the Scattered Squirrel link above if you need to make planners with the class (make sure to allot sufficient time for this- unless you have students do this prep work at home).
- Once students have their planners out, give them some time to set up or organize their own planner according to the checklist and then check off each checklist item.
- Remind students to use their planner daily.

Alternate Activity

If your students are very young, you may want to skip the planner work. In that case, you might just play a simplified version of the following School Success Bingo game. To simplify the game, give students bingo boards that are already filled in with only the first 5-10 strategies from the attached list. Go over the strategies with them before the game to briefly explain each one. You can also use this activity in place of the planner lesson if your distance learning environment makes the planner work too difficult. In that case, instruct students on how to play the bingo game with their families; after the family game, have students write, say, or draw a summary of their family bingo experience and submit it to you.

The Planner Checklist

Student Directions: Review each step below to set up your planner or agenda book. Then, to optimally use your planner as the efficient tool that it is, check off each step as you do it. Happy Planning!

My PLANNER has:
- ☐ **My name written on the planner cover.**
- ☐ **An assignment or "none" written for every subject.**
- ☐ **No major rips, bends, or graffiti on/in it.**
- ☐ **Every weekday filled in with assignments.**
- ☐ **Finished assignments that are crossed out or checked off.**

May's Theme:
Review of Skills Learned &
Wishes for the Future

American School Counselor Association Standards Alignment
Mindsets
M 2. Self-confidence in ability to succeed
Behaviors
B-LS 2. Demonstrate creativity
B-LS 5. Apply media and technology skills
B-SMS 7. Demonstrate effective coping skills when faced with a problem
B-SMS 10. Demonstrate ability to manage transitions and ability to adapt to changing situations and responsibilities

Objectives
The student will:
- Explore healthy coping skills as a mental health support strategy.
- Analyze how their current grades will affect their future college experience.
- Define emergencies and identify how to get help in an emergency situation.
- Reflect on what they learned this year through a review and guidance curriculum posttest.
- Identify hopes and wishes for the next school year.

Materials
- Printables from August Lesson: Posttest, Do You Have an Emergency? posterette, Request to See the Counselor forms/instructions, Four Steps of Conflict Resolution posterette
- *I Wish You More* by Amy Krouse Rosenthal, drawing paper, pencils, crayons, markers, needs assessments, chart paper and markers, internet with laptop or projector to show Jonard's story @ https://bigfuture.collegeboard.org/get-started/student-profile/meet-jonard, laptops or tablets for students to use with internet connection so they can access Big Future's Academic Tracker @ https://bigfuture.collegeboard.org/get-in/your-high-school-record/are-you-on-track-to-get-in-academic-tracker

Lesson Steps
DAY ONE

1. Introduction (5 min): Reintroduce yourself by stating your name and your role in the school. Review how students can fill out a Request to See the Counselor form/instructions, if necessary. Show the Do You Have an Emergency? posterette to review or explain what defines an emergency. Tell students that they should come to your office immediately if they have an emergency and that they don't need to fill out a request form for emergencies. Remind them that every adult in the school building must work with another adult/s if students tell them of a "3 hurts" emergency; this is because the top priority is to keep students safe.

2. Opening Activity (10 min): Brainstorm with students all the different mental health support strategies they have learned about in guidance lessons this year (i.e., self hug, get good grades, eat healthy, etc.) and write their answers down in a list on chart paper.
   Alternately, if this is the first mental health support strategy that you are teaching this year, define this term (healthful strategies that help us get through the emotionally tough times in our lives) and then have students brainstorm different things they could do to boost their mental health during times of stress or conflict. Write their answers down in a list on chart paper.
   Tell students that they have just made a list of healthy coping skills (HCS) and explain that these are the healthy things we do to feel better when we have a problem or feel bad. Title the chart list "Healthy Coping Skills". Tell them that we will identify our favorite HCS today and also discuss college life as another HCS we can look forward to in our future!

3. Mental Health Support Strategy- Healthy Coping Skills (10 min): Ask students what they think an unhealthy coping skill is and ask for some examples (fighting or yelling to express anger, smoking to reduce stress, etc.). Guide students to the idea that an unhealthy coping skill always leads to a second problem (such as suspension from school, lung cancer, etc.) in addition to the current problem or negative feeling that is making the person seek out a coping skill in the first place! Show students the attached list of HCS that we have learned this year (or use their brainstormed list in the Opening Activity if they identified all 15 of them) and briefly review each one. Have students determine their favorite HCS from the list and hold up a finger number to show the number of their favorite HCS. Finally have a few students explain why it is their favorite.

4. Academic Success Strategy- Will Your Grades Get You Into College? (30 min): Ask students how imagining an exciting future that includes going to college could be another healthy coping skill. Explain that you will show them a video clip of a college student named Jonard, who felt very excited about his college experience. Jonard's college student video can be found at https://bigfuture.collegeboard.org/get-started/student-profile/meet-jonard. After the video clip, follow these steps:

a) Briefly review (or introduce) the idea that college includes any learning institution after high school, such as a 2-year community college, a 4-year university, a trade school, a training institute, etc.

b) Have students show a thumb up/down if Jonard's experience makes them interested or excited about attending some type of college after high school.

c) If necessary, explain briefly about how Jonard and all students must apply to attend a college and then the college reviews student grades as well as other factors to decide if they will accept that student into their college.

d) Next, ask students to think about their grades that they check on every week- have them show a thumb up/down if they think their grades will help them get into college.

e) Tell students that you will lead them through an activity that will help them to find out if they have the grades necessary to get into the college of their choice. Model for students how to use Big Future's Academic Tracker (follow steps 1-4 at this link): https://bigfuture.collegeboard.org/get-in/your-high-school-record/are-you-on-track-to-get-in-academic-tracker. Then give the students a chance to try the tracker out on their own.

f) Use the following questions to process and wrap up the activity:
  • If your grades are lower than your college's expectations, how could you bring your grades up to your college's expectations? (ex- study nightly, go to tutoring, take better notes, organize your binder/backpack/planner, etc.)
  • How could you incorporate these above tasks into a grade improvement plan?
  • What steps would you take to work on your grade improvement plan every day?

If the Big Future Tracker activity is too mature for your students, feel free to skip Steps D/E. Instead, brainstorm some ideas with the class on how to create a plan to improve grades if students feel they need better ones to get into college.

5. Closure (5 min): Wrap up the lesson by having each student tell a partner their favorite HCS.

6. Lesson Evaluation (5 min): Have students do a thumbs up-thumbs down lesson evaluation with you while you read them each of the following evaluation statements:
  • I understood this lesson.
  • I know how to use my favorite HCS to feel better in a healthful way.
  • I enjoyed this lesson.
  • I know how grades affect college admission.

DAY TWO

The inclusion of a posttest and needs assessment in Day Two of this lesson give it a 90-minute run time. If that is too long for your situation, consider giving the posttest and needs assessment in a separate lesson (possibly in a June guidance lesson activity/time slot, if your school year runs that long).

1. Introduction (5 min): Reintroduce yourself by stating your name and your role in the school. Review how students can fill out a Request to See the Counselor form in order to meet with you to talk about any problem they are having. Show the Do You Have an Emergency? poster to review or explain what defines an emergency. Tell students that they should come to your office immediately if they have an emergency and that they don't need to fill out a request form for emergencies. Remind them that every adult in the school building is a mandated reporter and what this means for confidentiality.

2. Opening Activity (5 min): Explain to students that this will be the last guidance lesson of the school year, since summer break is coming soon! Ask students how they are feeling about school ending for the year.

3. Connection to Day One Activity- Endings & Healthy Coping Skills (5 min): Tell students that reflecting on their wishes and hopes for the next stage of their life can be a HCS to deal with the sadness of an ending. Explain that this is because hopes for the future lift us up rather than getting bogged down with the negative feelings that something is ending. Now, have everyone turn to a partner and tell them one unhealthy coping skill to avoid if someone is sad because of an ending in their life.

4. Summer Wish Activity (30 min): Tell students that people reflect on their wishes and hopes at the end of the school year since it is a time of endings and new beginnings. Explain that we will be reading a book together in this last guidance lesson that explores different kinds of wishes. Show students the book, *I Wish You More*, and ask them what they think the story is about. Read the book aloud to the class; even though it is a picture book, its themes and enchanting illustrations make it absolutely appropriate for secondary students as well as elementary students. Once you have finished reading the story, give the students blank paper and have them draw and color their wish for the summer.

5. Review and Posttest (15 min): Give the class a minute of think time to reflect on the main points that they learned in guidance lessons this year. Write their ideas on chart paper, making sure they are able to cover the topics listed on the posttest (if not, you'll probably need to reteach that topic before giving the posttest or remove it from the posttest if it was not applicable to your guidance curriculum). Next, have the students complete the attached posttest, either electronically (through Google Forms) or in a paper-based form. No matter the age, it is best to read the posttest aloud as they complete it- doing so prevents reading issues from impacting guidance data.

6. Needs Assessment (10 min): Follow the directions in the attached Needs Assessment to administer it to the students. The results will show what you can remove or add to this/your guidance curriculum next year, based on your students' perceptions of their own needs.

7. Conflict Resolution Practice (5 min): If time, do a final conflict resolution role play by following these steps:
   - Review the 4 steps of Conflict resolution a final time with the class.
   - Choose one student volunteer to act out the 4 Steps of Conflict Resolution while you, or another student "bother" them in a minor way.

8. Closure (10 min): Wrap up the lesson by having students do a Gallery Walk to view and share thoughts on each other's wish drawings.

9. Evaluation (5 min): End the lesson with a quick class evaluation. Have students do a thumbs up-thumbs down lesson evaluation with you while you read them each of the following statements:
   - I understood today's lesson.
   - I enjoyed today's lesson.
   - I have wishes and hopes for my future.

Healthy Coping Skills

Student Question: Which one do you use to make yourself feel better?

1. Talk to someone about your problems and feelings.
2. Exercise.
3. Meditate or do relaxation exercises such as grounding.
4. Spend time with your pet(s).
5. Eat well and sleep well.
6. Get help from the school counselor or another trusted adult.
7. Get good grades.
8. Have an attitude of gratitude.
9. Walk away from someone who is bothering you
10. Use an "I" message to tell someone how you feel.
11. Help others to feel hopeful.
12. Spend time connecting with other people.
13. Practice good time management.
14. Prioritize your tasks.
15. Listen to music.

Guidance Curriculum Needs Assessment

<u>Counselor Information:</u> Guidance curriculum needs assessments are an absolute necessity for planning next year's curriculum. Using Google Forms, administer the needs assessment during that same final guidance lesson of the year- you can even combine the posttest and needs assessment into one form for simultaneous data collecting. It is important to utilize a needs assessment in order to have student-driven data on what topics to plan next year's guidance lessons around. It is also fine to do the needs assessment at the beginning of the school year, but it is such a busy time of year, that it's best save it for the end and then just use that data for the following year (which will be only 2 months away). You can also use the resource below as is in the form of a paper-based survey which works well too, though it is much more time-consuming to analyze and compile paper-based data.

**If you are using this resource with elementary students, it is best to reduce the questions and topics by at least half.

Following is the needs assessment; feel free to print it out and use as is or turn it into a Google Form, Survey Monkey, or any other medium of your choice. Happy Data Collecting!

Student Needs Assessment

Student Directions: Here are some topics that we might explore in future guidance lessons. Please put a check under the YES column if you want/need to learn about the topic -OR- put a check in the NO column if you don't want/need to learn about the topic.

Guidance Topics	YES, I want/need to learn about this topic.	NO, I don't want/need to learn about this topic.
Conflict Resolution		
Friendship Issues		
Child Abuse Prevention		
Getting Help in Emergencies		
How to See your Counselor		
Social Media Issues		
Drug/Alcohol Problems		
Improving your Grades		
Improving your Behavior		
Avoiding Gossip/Rumors		
Anger Management Strategies		
Stress Management Strategies		
Handling Test Anxiety		
Going to College		
Paying for College		
Handling Family Problems		

References

If you would like to learn more about any of the strategies or activities in this counseling guide, please refer to the sources below.

American School Counselor Association. (2019). *The ASCA National Model: A Framework for School Counseling Programs, Fourth Edition.* Alexandria, VA: Author.

American School Counselor Association. (2016). *The School Counselor and Trauma Informed Practice.* Retrieved from https://www.schoolcounselor.org/asca/media/asca/PositionStatements/PS_TraumaInformed.pdf

American School Counselor Association. (2014). *The School Counselor and Multitiered System of Supports.* Retrieved from https://www.schoolcounselor.org/asca/media/asca/PositionStatements/PS_MTSS.pdf

AmericanSPCC.org. (2019). *Child abuse statistics.* Retrieved from https://americanspcc.org/child-abuse-statistics/

Big Future. (2019). *Jonard's story.* Retrieved from https://bigfuture.collegeboard.org/get-started/student-profile/meet-jonard

Big Future. (2019). *Academic tracker.* Retrieved from https://bigfuture.collegeboard.org/get-in/your-high-school-record/are-you-on-track-to-get-in-academic-tracker

Bologna, C. (2019). *6-year-old says no to bullying with sweet back-to-school shirt.* Retrieved from https://www.huffpost.com/entry/6-year-old-bullying-back-to-school-shirt_l_5d483e61e4b0aca341218094

CASEL.org. (2020). *SEL in action.* Retrieved from https://casel.org/in-action/

Centers for Disease Control and Prevention. (2019). *Death rates due to suicide and homicide among persons Aged 10–24.* Retrieved from https://www.cdc.gov/nchs/data/databriefs/db352-h.pdf

Cidlik, M. (2013). *Thankful.* Retrieved from https://www.familyfriendpoems.com/poem/thankful-for-life

CNN. (2016). *Avoid skipping meals.* Retrieved from http://www.YouTube.com/watch?v=DsXSXHurYCI

College Board. (2011). *Five ways ed pays.* Retrieved from https://www.YouTube.com/watch?v=spNDLD2KRuA

College Board. (2019). *Learn more, earn more.* Retrieved from https://bigfuture.collegeboard.org/get-started/know-yourself/learn-more-earn-more

College Board. (2011). *You Can Go to College.* Retrieved from https://www.YouTube.com/watch?v=3J7AvMFifR8

Kaffenberger, C. (2013). *Making Data Work Third Edition.* Alexandria, VA: American School Counselor Association.

Kidshealth.org. (2019). *How the body works: Your weight. Retrieved from* https://kidshealth.org/en/kids/healthy-weight-movie.html?WT.ac=ctg#catmovies

Mayo Clinic. (2018). *Mental illness in children.* Retrieved from https://www.mayoclinic.org/healthy-lifestyle/childrens-health/in-depth/mental-illness-in-children/art-20046577

Morin, A. (2015). *Seven scientifically proven benefits of gratitude.* Retrieved from https://www.psychologytoday.com/us/blog/what-mentally-strong-people-dont-do/201504/7-scientifically-proven-benefits-gratitude

NAMI.org. (2019). *Mental health by the numbers.* Retrieved from https://www.nami.org/learn-more/mental-health-by-the-numbers

National Association of School Psychologists. (2015). *Recommended Books for Children Coping with Loss or Trauma.* Retrieved from https://www.nasponline.org/x33507.xml

O'Brien, N. (2019). *9 highest paying jobs without a [4 year] college degree.* Retrieved from https://youtu.be/NcKXxJ0XdAI

O'net. (2019). Retrieved from www.onetonline.org

Prevention.com. (2019) *Celebrities with depression.* Retrieved from https://www.prevention.com/health/mental-health/g20078276/celebrities-with-depression/#

Scatteredsquirrel.com. (2019). *Weekly planner printables.* Retrieved from https://scatteredsquirrel.com/printable/personal-planner/weekly-planner-printables/

Sesame Street. (2012). *Sesame Street: Sonia Sotomayor and Abby – Career.* Retrieved from https://www.YouTube.com/watch?v=EHICz5MYxNQ

School Superintendents Association [AASA]. (2018). *National college and career readiness indicators.* Retrieved from https://www.redefiningready.org/life-ready

MORE BOOKS BY STEPHANIE LERNER

Helping in Hard Places: Trauma-Informed School Counseling

School Counselor Side Hustle (co-authored with Dr. Russell Sabella)

Get Your Group On Volume One: Multi Topic Small Group Counseling Guides

Get Your Group On Volume Two: Multi Topic Small Group Counseling Guides

SMART Guidance 6Pak for Middle Schoolers

The Calm Downers: Anger Management Group Counseling Sessions Guide with Activities

¡Tranquila! Anger Management Counseling Guide with Spanish/English Activities

Where There's a Goal, There's a Way: Individual Counseling Sessions Guide with Activities

¡GOL! Individual Counseling Sessions Guide with Spanish/English Activities

Cope Into Hope: Individual Grief Counseling Guide with Activities

Bilingual Cope Into Hope: Individual Grief Counseling Guide with Spanish/English Activities

The Broken Hearts Club: Grief Group Counseling Guide

The Girl Project: Girl Group Counseling Guide

Charla Entre Chicas: Bilingual Girl Group Counseling Guide with Spanish/English Activities

Relajate: Bilingual Stress Management Group Counseling Guide with Spanish/English Activities

Goals Make the Man: Boys Leadership Group Counseling Guide

The Complete ESL for Beginners: Lessons Guide with Activities

The Complete ESL in the Middle: Intermediate English Lessons Guide

ESL for Beginners: Lessons Guide with Activities, Volume One

ESL for Beginners: Lessons Guide with Activities, Volume Two

ESL for Beginners: Lessons Guide with Activities, Volume Three

ESL in the Middle, Volume One: Intermediate English Lessons Guide with Activities

ESL in the Middle, Volume Two: Intermediate English Lessons Guide with Activities

ESL for Beginners – Culture Explorers

ESL Survival Skills – Exploring US Culture

ESL Express: Lessons Guide for Teaching Beginning English

***

For information and previews of my books, visit www.schoolcounselorstephanie.com.

Follow me at the sites below to receive info about my other upcoming books.
Website & Blog- www.schoolcounselorstephanie.com/
Facebook- www.facebook.com/schoolcounselorstephanie/
Instagram- www.instagram.com/schoolcounselorstephanie/
Pinterest- www.pinterest.com/schoolcounselorstephanie/

About the Author

Stephanie Lerner is a Johns Hopkins University-trained educator. She holds a BS in elementary education and an MS in counseling. With more than 20 years in both public and private education, she has Texas certifications in school counseling and bilingual/Spanish education. After traveling the world and teaching in such far off places as Mozambique and Bolivia, Stephanie came home to the United States to be a bilingual counselor and teacher in a high-need public school system. She is currently the school counselor program manager for the Texas Education Agency. When she's not writing, educating, or counseling, she enjoys ranch life with her husband and their menagerie of pets—all of whom practice healthy coping skills, of course!

Made in the USA
Middletown, DE
08 October 2020